The Church Of Power

The Church Of Power

*The Invincible Movement of the Christian Church
Through An Upside Down World According to
The Acts of the Apostles*

Completely Revised With
Two New Exciting Chapters

by

AMOS JONES, JR.

Towsend Press

Sunday School Publishing Board
NBC, USA, INC.
330 Charlotte Avenue
Nashville, Tennessee 37201-1188
1995

© 1995 by Dr. Amos Jones, Jr. All rights reserved.
Published by Townsend Press of the
Sunday School Publishing Board, NBC, USA, Inc.,
330 Charlotte Avenue,
Nashville, Tennessee 37201-1188

Unless otherwise marked, all Scripture references are taken from the Authorized Edition of the King James Version of the Bible, A. D. 1611. Greek references are taken from the Nestle-Aland Greek text.

PRINTED IN THE UNITED STATES OF AMERICA

Library of Congress Cataloging-in-Publication Data
Jones, Amos.
    The church of power : the invincible movement of the Christian church through an upside down world : completely revised with two new exciting chapters on the Acts of the Apostles / by Amos Jones, Jr.
    p. cm.
    ISBN 0-9605592-0-5
    1. Church and the world--Biblical teaching. 2. Mission of the church--Biblical teaching. 3. Bible. N.T. Acts--Criticism, interpretation, etc. I. Title.
    BS2545.C553J66 1995
    262--dc20   94-23619
                                                                        CIP
Library of Congress Number: 93-071137

ALL RIGHTS RESERVED

To Dr. T. J. Jemison and Dr. C. A. W. Clark, both of whom have striven to bring the National Baptist Convention, USA, Inc., to truly be a church of power.

ἀλλὰ λήμψεσθε δύναμιν ἐπελθόντος τοῦ ἁγίου πνεύματος ἐφ' ὑμᾶς, καὶ ἔσεσθέ μου μάρτυρες ἔν τε Ἰερουσαλὴμ καὶ ἐν πάσῃ τῇ Ἰουδαίᾳ καὶ Σαμαρείᾳ καὶ ἕως ἐσχάτου τῆς γῆς.

Acts 1:8

CONTENTS

	Page
PREFACE TO REVISED EDITION	ix
PREFACE TO FIRST EDITION	xiii

A SERMON "The Macedonian Call"
        Acts 16:9-15 1

CHAPTER I
   The Setting Of The Church In The Acts Of
   The Apostles 11

CHAPTER II
   The Center Of Power For The Church 31

CHAPTER III
   Power As The Foundation Of The Church 51

CHAPTER IV
   The Church Of Power 73

CHAPTER V
   The Church Empowered By God-Ordained
   Ecclesiastical Order According to Acts 6:1-7 97

CHAPTER VI
   Power For The Church Through Common
   Sharing According To Acts 4:32 131

BIBLIOGRAPHY 149

Preface To Revised Edition

The 1981 edition of *The Church of Power* was my first effort at book publishing. It showed in that it was poorly crafted in terms of printing quality. The fact that I allowed such a poor printing job to surface into the public reading market reflected my naivete as a writer, having no knowledge of the hazards and subsequent embarrassment of setting a printed work before the public without making sure it is ready for such exposure.

When I received the finished product of the first edition from the printer, I was appalled at what I held in my hand. I read page after page of print which was blotched with one typographical error after another. There were footnote numbers which were cited within the body of the text on one page while the actual footnotes themselves appeared on another page, e.g., the previous page or the page following. In short, the entire book was an embarrassment to me, in terms of the poor quality of printing. Because the project was financed by me personally, I felt I could not afford to have the book reprinted, so, I conceded to the inevitable. Thus, I must take full and complete responsibility for what appeared in the first edition. For those of you who labored through that first edition, I congratulate you for the courage and apologize for your having to do so.

Having said this, I must say that I am very proud of what was said in the first edition of *The Church of Power*. Now after almost fourteen years since it first appeared, I can still say I am fascinated with the Acts of the Apostles.

As I have mused over the pages of the first edition of *The Church of Power*, inquiring about what I said and how I said it, I conclude that I really do not have much to add that is different from what I said in 1981, i.e., on the areas covered in that volume. I am even more convinced today that the church of the Acts of the Apostles was one which demonstrated herself in power through prayer, witnessing, and preaching the Word of God. I am even more-so convinced that when we compare the Early Church of the Acts of the Apostles with the contemporary Black Baptist church (and every other Black church of any denomination as far as that is concerned), we are weighed in the balance and found wanting. We are weak, puny, and powerless compared to the church of the Acts.

When I began to look seriously at the Acts of the Apostles while a student at Vanderbilt Divinity School in Nashville, I quite naturally did so by seeking out the thoughts and deposits of scholars. You will find infrequent references to some of these in the first edition. However, I have not seen the need to enter into dialogue with scholars as is the norm in academic circles. I am interested in reaching the millions of Christian educators, especially those of the National Baptist Convention, USA, Inc. Thus, it is not my interest to add to this work the heavy and obtuse freight of theological arguments and entangling jargon concerning form criticism, the historicity of this, or who wrote that. My interest is what the Acts of the Apostles can say to the church in general and the National Baptist church in general.

As I evaluated what was done in the first edition, there was so much which was omitted. As I have continued to look at the first edition, my conclusion is that there are a myriad of subjects which could and maybe even should be included in such a book. Not enough can be said concerning the fact that the New Testament Early Church was a power, a force, a dynamic movement, a monolith of multiples to be dealt with in her time and over the course of history. For example, my several journeys to Israel have caused Caesarea on the Mediterranean to leap out at me as a most significant location in the Acts of the Apostles. It is there to which Philip went after he preached the gospel to and baptized the Ethiopian Eunuch. Peter went there after his vision on the housetop at Joppa. At Caesarea, he evangelized the Roman Centurion Cornelius. Last, but surely not least, it was there that Paul the Apostle was carried as a prisoner to appear before Herod and King Agrippa. In the outdoor theater is where he stood on the stage in chains and preached of Jesus Christ and caused Agrippa to say, "Almost you have persuaded me to be a Christian." My journeys to Israel have caused me to conclude that the Acts of the Apostles is very historical, laden with places which are extant even to this day.

As I approached the revision of this book, my judgment was that you have to stop somewhere. Many of the foci which leap out at you when you study carefully the Acts of the Apostles will simply have to be treated in another publication approaching them from another angle. However, I have concluded that in order to make the point of the power of the Early Church, there is the need to include in the revised edition something on the strength of the church's organization and finances, according to the Acts of the Apostles. Two phases of church life which reflect terrible weakness within National Baptist churches are 1) lack of organizational strength due to friction and impasse between the pastor and deacons and 2) poor stewardship which factors out in the failure of National Baptist churches to meet their financial potential, a potential which would permit them to meet many of the pressing needs of the eight million who claim membership. I have included a chapter on the relationship of the deacon with that of the pastor, or the apostles as was the case in the days of the church of the

Acts of the Apostles. Also, I was always impressed with the economic independence of the Early Church, an independence which manifested itself in strength to resist the Roman Empire. Hence, I have included a chapter exploring the question of how the Early Church of the Acts of the Apostles acquired power through economic strength and independence. With a great deal of faith and tremendous stretch of the imagination, it is my hope that we can catch the spirit of the Early Church and gain some measure of its expertise in stewardship so that we too can become a church of financial power.

It is my sincere opinion that there are numerous subjects which could be treated to reinforce the idea of the Early Church as a church of power. Having added the two new chapters, it is not my intention to add anything else to what I have written herein.

The intention of all this is to challenge National Baptist churches to emulate the church of the Acts of the Apostles, i.e., to strive to become a church of power. There is no better time than now for the Negro Baptist church to manifest herself as a strong representative of the Christian Community which offers powerful answers and solutions to today's gripping problems which we face as Black and poor people.

The first edition provided a great service to thousands of National Baptists. I hope this edition enjoys the same good graces. It is with this intention, accompanied by the grace of God, that I offer the book to you.

Preface

In the pages that follow, the reader is invited to ponder what is at this time that which represents the depth of my thought and the height of my understanding of the Acts of the Apostles. The four chapters are the result of four lectures which were delivered at the Tennessee Baptist Leadership Education Congress in July of 1978 at the Macedonia Baptist Church of Jackson, Tennessee. The four chapters in particular are the product of a refinement process which came about after addressing myself to the questions directed to me from ministers and members of the Ministers' Seminar where the lectures were delivered during the 1978 Tennessee Baptist State Congress. Included also in this publication is a sermon which was preached in a series of messages from the Acts of the Apostles delivered at Westwood Baptist Church, University Center in Nashville, Tennessee over a period of a year and a half. A bibliography of commentaries, books, and articles has been included to facilitate the Bible student's or minister's study of the Acts of the Apostles.

For the first few years of my career, as one who has attempted to ponder deeply the meaning of New Testament writings, the Acts of the Apostles remained enshrouded in complete mystery and enigma. I gravitated toward Pauline studies and became quite an avid student of the Apostle to the Gentiles. Studying Paul and his writings caused me to set beside him and his writings the Acts of the Apostles, for much is said in the Acts of the Apostles about Paul. There surfaced within me a personal dislike for the Acts of the

Apostles because of what I discovered to be disparities between its account of Paul's life and the accounts given by The Apostle himself in his writings. For example, Roman citizenship for Paul is clearly stated in Luke's version of The Apostle's biography in chapter sixteen of Acts, but in his own biography in chapter three of Philippians there is no hint of Roman citizenship. There are clear discrepancies in the sequence of activities that follow Paul's conversion. For example, in the Acts he goes first to Damascus where he meets with Ananias and then to Jerusalem where his calling is confirmed by the brethren of the congregation there. In contradistinction, Paul tells the Galatians that he met with no man when he was called by God to preach the Gospel but immediately went to Arabia. Yet another disparity is that Paul in Acts was an eloquent speaker, but not a writer of letters. On the other hand, Paul of the Pauline letters was not considered anything more than a mediocre speaker but was feared for his ability to write letters (2 Cor. 10:10). These were just some of the disparities I discovered between the Acts of the Apostles and the genuine Pauline letters of the New Testament. These initially generated within me a disfavor for the book.

A dramatic turning point for me and my appreciation for the Acts of the Apostles was my encounter with the New Testament scholar, Martin Dibelius. Becoming acquainted with his position on The Acts through his writings, he postulated that the Acts of the Apostles was **Lukan historiography**. By this, Dibelius meant that Luke wrote the Acts of The Apostles although he was not an eyewitness of the actual development of the Early Church. He set down in writing what the Holy Spirit led him to believe was the best report of the beginnings of the church. Especially did Luke shape the story in a way that was best for the church. Giving shape, flavor, and color to history, i.e., telling the story from the writer's point of view, albeit some of the details were not altogether historical, hence, historiography, was commonly a characteristic of writers of history in Luke's day.

Another feature of the Acts of the Apostles which commanded my appreciation was that it was a theological, as well as political apology. Luke's version of the historical beginnings of the church was his attempt to say to the reader that The Christian Faith was/is the most genuine of all religions. He shows this in many ways, viz., the tremendous growth of the church in spite of opposition; the power of the apostles to withstand persecution for the sake of the Name of Jesus; the power of the apostles to heal those who were sick, and the like. As a political apology, the Acts of the Apostles is Luke's attempt to say to the Roman world about him that the church is not a threat to the Roman Empire. Although this is what one would conclude from a surface reading of the book, a different conclusion is drawn when one plumbs the depths of Luke's mind and sets what he has written in the midst of the actual history of his day.

These two features of the Acts of the Apostles have convinced me that it is a most radical presentation of the beginnings of the Early Church. The Acts of The Apostles rises up before us anew as a challenge to the contemporary church to be like the church of the Acts of the Apostles. **Therefore, I simply have attempted to tell the story once again, trying to capture Luke's intent**. I have begun by setting the scenario, the historical setting, of the stage on which the Early Church began her movement. The discussion tries to capture the righteous contempt held by the disciples for the kinds of things that were going on in the Roman society about them. It also tries to sense the power and force by which Jesus launched the church from the Mt. of Olives. Focussing on the first few chapters of the Acts of the Apostles, the discussion attempts to lift several of the salient factors that made the Early Church an unstoppable movement. We try to monitor carefully these movements and lift at every point the challenge they present to the church of today.

Today's society is very much like that in which the members of the Early Church found themselves. The church of today, like the church of the Acts of the Apostles, is faced once again with the question of whether the Lord now is ready to set things right in this world. The inevitable response from heaven is the same which was spoken on the slopes of Mt. Olive and that is that the world will be better and the situation will change for the best and the church will be the reason for it all. This will be the case because God will make use of the church as an instrument in His hands to cut through the thicket and tangled maze of sin a path for all who are willing to travel it.

It is my hope that like myself, the reader will be challenged by the Acts of the Apostles to see the role of the church in a new and powerful light. More than this, it is my hope that the reader will allow the contemporary church to become once again an instrument in the hands of God, as it was in the Acts of the Apostles, and thereby become a powerful force of righteousness and salvation in this world.

I wish to thank the Reverend Dr. Reuben H. Green, Dean of the Tennessee Baptist Leadership Education Congress, for extending me the invitation to be guest lecturer for the 1978 session. I also thank the Reverend Nesbie Alston, President of the Tennessee Baptist Leadership Education Congress, for his leadership and support. I am extremely grateful for the questions raised by the ministers and members of the Ministers' Seminar of the 1978 Congress session, an auxiliary of the Tennessee Baptist Missionary and Education Convention, for they listened intently to these lectures and raised some very important questions. Their questions and verbal expressions of appreciation motivated me to formally put these ideas in print. My appreciation is unlimited for the faculty and staff at the American Baptist College and Vanderbilt Divinity School. Especially am I grateful to Dr. Leander E. Keck, formerly of Vanderbilt Divinity School, for putting me on a good foundation for New Testament study. I am deeply indebted to the members of the Westwood Baptist Church, University Center, Nashville, Tennessee, for they listened for one year and a half to my preaching from the Acts of the Apostles. So in sermon form, the members of the congregation I have pastored for the last eleven years have heard the contents of these lectures. Finally, I am completely lost for words to express my appreciation and indebtedness to my wife Grace, and our daughter Sabrina and her children, Carey and Janee. The days have been many when I have been merely like a passing shadow, coming in from a long day of pounding a pastor's beat, stopping only briefly to get a kiss and say hello and then going quickly to my study to work on lectures such as these. I must set down in print for these who are dearest to me how much I appreciate their sacrifice.

I extend a word of appreciation to Darden Printing Company of Nashville, Tennessee for publishing these lectures. However, I must be held personally responsible for all errors of print and statements made herein.

A SERMON
"THE MACEDONIAN CALL"
Acts 16:9-15

Chapter sixteen of the Acts of the Apostles is like a great hinge that swings wide a door which carries the Gospel of Jesus Christ onto the broad continent of Europe. In verse nine of the sixteenth chapter, the location of our text, Paul sees a vision of a man crying in the night, "Come over to Macedonia and help us."

As Paul and Silas sought to begin their second missionary journey, Luke says that they sought to go into Bithynia; but, he says, ". . .the Spirit of Jesus did not allow them" (Acts 16:7 RSV). It can be concluded from what is said here that what a church wants to do is not all the time what the Holy Spirit wants it to do. Paul and Silas wanted to go into Bithynia, but the Holy Spirit had them to know that their priorities were mixed up. There was a situation in Macedonia where somebody needed them worse than in Bithynia. So while passing through Mysia and going down to Troas, Paul saw a vision in the night of a man who was lifting up a wail and cry, "Come over to Macedonia and help us!" It could be that the church today is so busy doing its own thing, and so busy going in its own direction, operating on its own plan rather than the plan of God, that it cannot be guided by the plan of the Holy Spirit; and, it cannot hear the Macedonian Call for someone to come over and help. All too often, the church is more concerned with raising the budget than it is with raising somebody's bowed down head. The Bible says that when Paul saw the vision of the man crying in the night, "...immediately we sought to go on into Macedonia, concluding that God had called us to preach the gospel to them" (Acts 16:10 RSV).

So it was that a cry went up in the night for Paul and his companion, representatives of a church with a center of power, to "Come over to Macedonia and help us." But why this call of distress from the land of Macedonia? What problem in Macedonia was so pressing that the travel arrangements of the apostles had to be changed by the Holy Spirit so they should go there and see about it? Well, maybe a look at Macedonia itself will give us the answer.

Macedonia, situated on the grand elevation of the Pangean Range, overlooked the luscious green-watered plains of Asia Minor. This great nation, founded by the unmatched Philip of Macedon, was characterized as having a reserve of moral as well as material strength. Under the leadership of Philip, Macedonia came to be known as a region towering o'er her national neighbors as probably the "most honest, the most serious, the most pious of the ancient world."

This was great Macedonia. But in 168 B.C., something happened to Macedonia; Macedonia was conquered by the awesome might of the Roman Empire. And, when Rome moved in, righteousness moved out. For Rome broke up the unity of Macedonia and divided the nation into four districts, of which Philippi was the leading city of what now became a Roman colony. Macedonia, that once was united, now was divided. They divided up Macedonia then, like they divide up the inner city in America today by running interstate highways through the ghettoes of our cities, dividing the communities of Black people. But something more vicious than this happened in Macedonia and Philippi, its chief city; for not only did Rome divide the nation of Macedonia, it divided its entire lifestyle. Families were divided; and, brother was pitted against brother; and, sister was pitted against sister. Children were urged to rise up against their parents. Husbands and wives were separated from each other. It was an attack against the basic unit in society, the family. It was an exercise of what Michael Grant calls in his book *The World of Rome,* "divide and conquer."

Even though Rome had given the city of Philippi the false security of *libertas* (the ability of self-government), and *immunitas* (freedom from paying taxes), and *ius Italicum* (the privileges of the city of Rome itself), **there really was neither joy nor security in Philippi; for as its nation was broken, so were its families and people broken.** So out of the hell of that brokenness in Philippi, went up a blood-curdling cry in the night to those couriers of the Gospel, "Come over to Macedonia and help us."

The Macedonian Call goes out from the cities of this nation, America. All across this great nation of ours are cities and hamlets which stand in the radiant splendor of success and promenade in the gleaming promise of prosperity, but out of whose bosoms rise the awful wail and cry in the night, "Come over to Macedonia and help us." New York City, wallowing in the riches of Wall Street; Washington, D. C., the national seat of political deliberation; Philadelphia, the City of Brotherly Love; Pittsburgh, the steel capital of the nation; Carl Sandburg's Chicago, meat packer of the nation and hub of world travel; St. Louis, the gateway to the West; Memphis, home of the blues; New Orleans, rocking to the rhythm of ragtime; Houston and Dallas/Ft. Worth, rich in money from the sale of cattle and oil; Denver, the mile-high city with breath-taking brilliance; Los Angeles, the city of movie stars and the city of angels; and then there is San Francisco, the city that sits majestically on the curvaceous hills of Northern California, kissed by the cooling currents of a Pacific breeze. In all of these cities, there seems to be peace and prosperity. But from the blistering ghettoes of all of these cities, from every sleepy village and hamlet that dots the hillsides of our nation, there rises in the night of desperation a shrieking cry for somebody to "come over here and help us." For over here, there is crime in the streets and crime in the suites. Over here, there is crime in the courtroom and crime in the living room. Over here, there is poverty and pain, sickness and suffering. Over here, our young people are high on drugs and our old people are high on drink. Over here, our marriages are breaking up and our families are breaking down. "Come over here and help us" goes up the piercing cry in the night from every location in the nation.

As the cry goes up in the nation, the church cannot repose in the comfort of its sanctity and the quiet of its cloister. The church must respond and address itself to the horrors of the night that hold captive the sons of men. Paul and Silas, representing the church, heard the wail and cry that went up in Philippi that night. The record says that ". . .immediately we sought to go on into Macedonia, concluding that God had called us to preach the gospel to them." When Paul and Silas had sailed into Samothrace, and had gone the following day to Neapolis, and had finally come to Philippi, they went to the heart of the problem which was troubling the souls of the people, the division of the family. Paul and Silas went to address the Gospel to the problem of the broken home.

Notice here that Paul did not address himself to the government of Rome and the false security that it offered to the people. I think he chose not to do this because the

Roman government was the greater part of the problem and certainly was not a part of the solution. The corruption of Roman government and the immorality of Roman lifestyle was the cause of the brokenness of Philippian life and the Philippian family. So, Paul sought to get at the root of the problem, work with and straighten out the crookedness of the broken home. In fact, this is the whole story of the sixteenth chapter of the Acts of the Apostles, that of the Gospel redeeming the family from the hell of brokenness. And I am convinced that if our cities and our society are going to be better, the noble process must begin with the family; for where there is a breakdown in the family, there is a breakdown in society. So the church must rise up to the occasion and answer the terrifying cry in the night to, "Come over here and help us!"

Just as Paul and Silas did not begin their noble redemptive process with the government in Philippi, we cannot begin the process with the government because it is, for the most part, not a part of the solution; it is a part of the problem. What of a police force that is part of the prostitution business that litters our streets and destroys the bodies of our young women? What of adult book stores and peep shows that contaminate the mind of the people? What of the FBI and CIA and the Mafia which superintend the conveyance of drugs into the communities about us, destroying the lives of our young people? What of the television industry that teaches our people to gamble by day, drink, curse and kill by night? No! We cannot begin with the government or anything else; we must begin with the family, the foundation of society.

Some years ago in Nashville, there was much discussion about a police maneuver called Operation Sting. There was concern about the appropriateness of how it was carried out. Young boys and girls, some of whom were children of prominent people, most of whom were Black, were caught and arrested for selling stolen merchandise. There was concern about the legitimacy and legality of the operation. Well, I am not so sure I am that concerned with the question of the legitimacy and the legality of the operation. I am more concerned with the question of why Black youth are engaged in wrongdoing in the first place. I am more concerned with the question of why Black parents do not know where their children are at night. I am more concerned with why Black mothers are bringing children into the world, failing to give them a foundation of faith in God and a guide that is drawn out of the deep resources of Jesus' moral and ethical teachings. I am more concerned about Black men who, more and more, are big enough to make a baby, but are not big enough to take care of a baby. I am concerned about Black men who increasingly are not marrying the love of their life and the mother of their children, and therefore are not providing their children, sons of their loins, the fatherly image and guidance they need. I am concerned about this for, you see, you cannot expect a child to go right when he has been raised wrong. I am concerned about the breakdown of the family.

Urie Bronfenbrenner, in an article in *Psychology Today*, says one of the major problems today is that of children coming home to an empty house; neither momma nor poppa is home when they come from school. So they, having nothing to do, find something to do with their time. They get in trouble! Our national statistics are that there are 28,500 young people in street gangs, and the vast majority of them are Black. You cannot expect a corrupt government to correct such a situation. The judge's correction in the courtroom can never replace a father's correction in the back room of the house and Bible teaching in the church house. If things are going to be better, they must begin with the family; and the church must be the performing force.

Paul took the Gospel to the heart of the problem, the family in Philippi. The fruit of the Gospel had already been born in the family on Paul's first missionary journey. While preaching in Lystra, one of the converts there was a young boy by the name of Timothy, who had come from a broken home. In the first three verses of this sixteenth chapter, Timothy's family is mentioned. His mother is spoken of as a believer; but of his father, the record only registers that he was a Greek. In the Second Epistle of Timothy, there is reference made to Timothy's grandmother, Lois, and his mother, Eunice; but, there is not a reference made to his father. The boy was raised in a broken home; this is my conclusion. But that did not matter, for his grandmother and mother taught him the scriptures from the days of his youth. The boy grew up to be decent and honorable. When Timothy heard the Gospel, he accepted the message and became a disciple of Jesus Christ. Verse two of this sixteenth chapter of the Acts of the Apostles says, "He was well spoken of by the brethren of Lystra and Iconium." Rather than grow up to be a problem in society, Timothy grew up to provide the solution for society by proclaiming the Gospel of Jesus Christ; and as such, he drew the admiration of all about him. The Gospel will do the same for youngsters today when parents allow it to influence their lives. The Gospel will lead a child aright. And you mother, trying to raise a child in a broken home, without a husband for yourself and a father for your child, the choice is yours, whether you will raise your child in the church-house or see him stand before a judge in a courthouse. The Bible says, "Train up a child in the way he should go and when he is old he will not depart from it." If you raise your child in the church-house, chances are that you will not see him stand before a judge in a courthouse and rot away in a jailhouse.

The story moves on! On the Sabbath, Paul and Silas went down to a riverside in Philippi to a place where prayer was to be made. When they got there, they found a group of women praying. Among them was a woman named Lydia, an industrious woman. She was a seller of purple goods, a woman who made a living for herself and her entire household for there was no husband to help. But Lydia would always find time to go to church where prayer was to be made. Something in her said that no matter how much money she made, she could not be rich enough nor could she raise her family right without God in her life. So she sought God for herself and her family.

Thank God for women like Lydia. Women of the likes of Lydia must be enshrined in the sacred halls of memory in the Archives of Eternity. It was then and always has been that women of the likes of Lydia were those who loved God deeply and dedicated themselves to His church. Women were devoted to Jesus and owned him as their Lord. They cared for the Lord out of the penury of their pocketbooks and prepared meals for him as Lydia did for Paul and Silas. Heaven can never forget the faithfulness of women like Lydia.

The story in the Acts of the Apostles is that Paul preached the Gospel of Jesus Christ to Lydia. He must have told her that Jesus left His bright and shining throne in Glory to come to this world of sin and shame. He must have exclaimed that the Lord left the world of light to come to this world of darkness. It is likely that Paul told Lydia of how Jesus came from the world of the living into a world of the dying. Undoubtedly, he told of how He came through forty-two generations of Adam and was born of the Virgin Mary, born in a manger in Bethlehem, in keeping with what was spoken by the prophets. Surely, he told of His similarity to Moses, how He was carried to Egypt to escape attempts against His life. Hardly could he have told his story unless he told of how Jesus walked the dusty Genessaret Plains and passed through every village and city on His way to Jerusalem; and, on His way He healed people of their sickness and forgave them of their sin. Finally, obviously, Paul's message climaxed with the Good News of what happened at Calvary. He told that on Friday, Jesus died for the sins of the world, and that He laid in the grave all night Friday night, all day Saturday and all night Saturday night; and when it seemed that death had overcome and hell had actually conquered, early on Sunday morning, Jesus rose in power and glory over death, hell, and the grave. When Paul opened the doors of the church with the words of Jesus, "Whosoever will, let him come," Lydia came forth.

The Bible says that when Lydia heard the Word of God as it was preached by Paul, the Lord opened her heart to give heed to what was said in the Gospel message. The story is that she was baptized in the name of the Father, in the name of the Son, and in the name of the Holy Spirit. But wait! Lydia was not satisfied with finding Christ for herself, she wanted Christ for all her family. She went home and got her household, her children, and her grandchildren and offered them to be baptized. She did not wait for her children to make up their mind to join the church. She did not wait for her sons and her daughters to decide if they wanted to be Christians. She must have said to them, "If the Gospel is good enough for me, it is good enough for my children." So she said to Paul, "Here are my children, Paul; I don't want them to wreck on the rocks of wretchedness of this world. I don't want them to live in brokenness all of their lives, your Gospel can make them whole. Take my children and baptize them Paul." The Bible says that Lydia and all of her household were baptized that very day.

Well my brothers and sisters, the church today must hear and answer the Macedonian Call. The church must tell mommas and daddies that if they are fearful for their children in this mean and cruel world; if they are trying to raise them all by themselves; and if they are becoming more than they can bear, tell them what they can do. They can bring their children to the church and put them in the hand of the Lord and the Lord will make everything all right. Tell them that the government cannot do it. Tell them that welfare systems cannot do it, and Juvenile Corrections cannot do it. But if they bring them to the church and turn them over into the hands of the Lord, the Lord will take care of them. I know what I am talking about. My mother took me when I was very young and introduced me to the church, and the church introduced me to Jesus, and Jesus introduced me to God the Father. Momma took me to church every Sunday. I did not understand it then. I saw her cry. I saw the people shouting. I heard them talking about the goodness of the Lord. But now, I know what it is all about, for the same Jesus who was my momma's Lord has become my Lord too. I have come to know for myself that the Lord will take care of you. He has brought me, He has taught me, He has kept me and has never left me. The church must tell the parents of this day that if they bring their children to the church and hand them over to the Lord, the Lord will take care of them.

And because of what the church has come to mean to me, I now can say,

I love Thy church, O Lord; Her walls before Thee stand
She is the apple of Thine eye; Engraven on Thine hand.

Chapter I

THE SETTING OF THE CHURCH IN THE ACTS OF THE APOSTLES

The Acts of the Apostles is the second of a two-volume work by the Evangelist Luke. The first of the two-volume set is the Gospel of Luke. The Gospel of Luke is his story of Jesus. He introduces the work to Theophilus, the one, it seems, to whom the first volume is written. He says:

> Inasmuch as many have undertaken to compile a narrative of the things which have been accomplished among us, just as they were delivered to us by those who from the beginning were eyewitnesses and ministers of the word, it seemed good to me also, having followed all things closely for some time past, to write an orderly account for you, most excellent Theophilus, that you may know the truth concerning the things of which you have been informed. (Luke 1:1-4 RSV)

The second book, the book of the Acts of the Apostles, is also addressed to Theophilus (Acts 1:1). The significance of both volumes being addressed to a certain Theophilus seems to be that they were to be read together. This probably was the case because on the one hand, the Gospel of Luke was the story of Jesus, and the other hand, the Acts of the Apostles, was the story of the Church. C.K. Barrett, writing in his essay, *Luke the Historian in Recent Study*, described the connection of the two volumes like this:

Since the ascension is for Luke both the end of the ministry of Jesus, in which His life finds the triumphant conclusion that gives it meaning, and the beginning of the Church, which makes the life of the Church both possible and intelligible, it follows that, in Luke's thought, the end of the story of Jesus is the Church; and, the story of Jesus is the beginning of the Church. In this proposition lies the distinctive characteristics of Luke's work.... He is not the close of all history, but the starting-point of a new kind of history, Church History, whose horizons are indefinitely remote. This is what Luke perceived, and this is what gives him his unique place in the New Testament. He is the Father of Church History; it had not occurred to any Christian before him that there was any such thing.[1]

So the Acts of the Apostles is the story of the Church which Jesus left to carry on the work of the Kingdom of God in the world after His ascension. The Acts then becomes, according to Barrett, the beginning of Church History, or the history of the Church.

Luke is considered by most scholars to be the writer of the Acts of the Apostles. In the second century, Luke was referred to as the author of the Acts of the Apostles by Early Church fathers such as Origen, Clement of Alexandria, Tertullian, and Irenaeus. In the fourth century, the celebrated Eusebius of Caesarea credited the writing of the Acts of the Apostles to Luke. In the third book of Eusebius' *Ecclesiastical History* he says:

...Luke was born at Antioch and by profession a physician being for the most part connected with Paul, and familiarly acquainted with the rest of the apostles, has left us in two inspired books, the institutes of that spiritual healing art which he obtained from them. One of

---
[1]C. K. Barrett, *Luke the Historian in Recent Study*, Facet Books, Biblical Series No. 24 (Philadelphia: Fortress Press, 1970), p. 57f.

these is his gospel, in which he testifies that he has recorded, "as those who were from the beginning eyewitness, and ministers of the word," delivered to him. Whom also, he says, he has in all things followed. The other is his Acts of the Apostles, which he composed, not from what he had heard from others, but from what he had seen himself.[2]

In the studies of Robert M. Grant (*A Historical Introduction to the New Testament*), the point is made that Luke was considered the author of the Acts of the Apostles by the second century Church Father, Irenaeus of Lyons. Irenaeus concluded that it must have been Luke who accompanied Paul in the "we" passages of Acts (cf., Acts 16:9-18; 20:5, 21:18; 27:1; 28:16), and must have gone with him to Rome and was imprisoned with him as indicated in Colossians 4:14 and 2 Timothy 4:11. It seems that early in church tradition it was commonly accepted that Luke was the author of both the Gospel and the Acts of the Apostles. On the basis of this information, it is reasonable enough to conclude that Luke was the author of the book we know today as the Acts of the Apostles.

There is much debate about when the Acts of the Apostles was written. C. K. Barrett says, "It is possible that Luke-Acts was written towards the close of the first century, probably not far from the date of the Fourth Gospel."[3] Werner Georg Kümmel, however, sets the dating of the Acts of the Apostles about A.D. 85.[4] The place of the writing of Acts is not settled. Upon the basis of the "we" passage tradition, Kümmel conjectures that the location of the writing of Acts could have been Rome. But Edgar J. Goodspeed considers that the location of the writing of

---
[2]Eusebius Pamphilus, *Ecclesiastical History*, Bk. III. Chpt. IV.
[3]Ibid., p. 62.
[4]Werner Georg Kümmel, *Introduction to the New Testament*. 14th Revised Edition. Translated by A. J. Mattill, Jr. (Nashville: Abingdon Press, 1966), p. 133.

Acts could have been Ephesus or a Pauline church in Macedonia, Achaia, or Asia Minor.

HISTORICAL SETTING OF ACTS

Since we will try to appropriate the meaning of the church in our historical setting today, it may be well to spend some time setting the historical scenario of the Acts of the Apostles which gives us the beginning of the history of the Early Church. Once we get a picture of the historical setting of the Early Church as it is described in the Acts, we should see the parallels between those times and the times in which the church exists today. Further, we should be able to more readily adopt the means by which the Early Church, the church of the Acts of the Apostles, made its impact on the world in the name and glory of God.

In A.D. 85, the approximate year the Acts of the Apostles was written, the Early Church found itself in politically painful and stressful times. The entire civilized world had fallen under the dominance of the Roman Empire. All the major cities of the world were under Roman rule. Athens, Corinth, Ephesus, Thessalonica, Philippi, Alexandria (Egypt), and even Jerusalem all had fallen under Roman dominance. The emperors and the mighty armies of the Roman Empire had conquered every city, province, and nation by means of what Michael Grant called, "Divide and Rule."[5]

The power of Rome began to flex its muscles against Jerusalem when it sacked the city in A.D. 70, and destroyed the Zealot fortress of Masada and killed those zealous Jews

---

[5]Michael Grant, *The World of Rome*. A Mentor Book. (New York: New American Library, 1960), p. 73.

who resisted unto death the Roman taxation and desecration of their homeland, Palestine. The Christian Church did not escape the brutal sanguinary of Roman oppression. It was during the reign of Emperor Nero, according to legend, that Peter and Paul were crucified upside down in the Imperial City of Rome. In the earliest documents of the New Testament, we do not get a complete picture of the brutality inflicted upon the Early Christian Church. We do get some information from writers of history outside of the New Testament. The Roman historian, Suetonius, secretary to Emperor Hadrian A.D. 117-138, writing in his *Lives of the Caesars*, refers to the expulsion of the Jews from Rome during the reign of the Emperor, Deified Claudius A.D. 41-54, when he said, "Since the Jews constantly made disturbances at the instigation of Chrestus [sic] he expelled them from Rome."[6] During the reign of the madman, Nero, Suetonius remarks that "Punishment was inflicted on the Christians, a class of men given to a new and mischievous superstition."[7] Another Roman historian, Tacitus, writes a fuller story of the persecution of Christians under Emperor Nero. Tacitus tells us that in order to scotch the rumor that Nero himself had set fire to Rome, the Emperor made a spectacle of Christians in order to cover up his own guilt. Tacitus writes:

> Therefore, to scotch the rumor, Nero substituted as culprits, and punished with the utmost refinements of cruelty, a class of men, loathed for their vices, whom the crowd styled Christians. Christus, the founder of the name, and undergone the death penalty in the reign of Tiberius, by sentence of the procurator Pontius Pilatus, and the pernicious superstition was checked for a moment, only to break out once more, not merely in Judea,

---
[6] Suetonius, *Lives of the Caesars*, Trans. by J. C. Rolfe. Loeb Classical Library. No. 38. (Cambridge, Massachusetts: Harvard University Press, 1970), Bk. V. Chp. XXV.
[7] Ibid., Bk. VI. Chp. XXVI.

the home of the disease, but in the capital itself, where all things horrible or shameful in the world collect and find a vogue. First, then, the confessed members of the sect were arrested; next, on their disclosures, vast numbers were convicted, not so much on the count of arson as for hatred of the human race. And derision accompanied their end: they were covered with wild beasts skins and torn to death by dogs; or they were fastened on crosses, and, when daylight failed were burned to serve as lamps by night. Nero had offered his Gardens for the spectacle, and gave an exhibition in his Circus, mixing with the crowd in the habit of a charioteer, or mounted on his car. Hence, in spite of guilt which had earned the most exemplary punishment, there arose a sentiment of pity, due to the impression that they were being sacrificed not for the welfare of the state but to the ferocity of a single man.[8]

Under the reigns of the emperors Galba, Otho, Vitellius, Vespasian, and Titus, there is little known of what persecution the Christian Church might have undergone during the period from A.D. 68-81. But under the reign of Emperor Domitian (A.D. 81-96), persecution of the Christian Church flourished anew and the hell of Rome came down upon her with more ferocity. It was Domitian who arrogantly commanded that subjects of the Roman Empire refer to him as Dominus et deus, "Our Master and our God."[9]

It is strongly suspected that it was against Domitian's attempt to deify himself by having the subjects refer to him as "Master" and "God" that the Gospel writer John of the New Testament had Thomas refer to Jesus, not Domitian, as "My Lord and My God" (John 20:28). The

---
[8]Tacitus, *Annals*. Trans. by J. Jackson. Loeb Classical Library. No 322. (Cambridge, Massachusetts: Harvard University Press, 1969), Bk. XV. Chp. XLIV.
[9] Suetonius, Ibid. Bk. VIII. Chp. XIII

brutality of Domitian's reign as it was directed against the Christians and the church is clearly seen in that apocalyptic book of the Revelation to John, when John was exiled to the Isle of Patmos for the sake of the Word of God. Incidentally, it was during the reign of the brutal Emperor Domitian, that the Acts of the Apostles was written.

One last reference we will make regarding the political climate in which the Early Church existed is to the letter of Pliny the Younger, Governor of Bithynia, to the Emperor Trajan (ca., A.D. 112) regarding what to do with Christians.

PLINY TO THE EMPEROR TRAJAN

It is my custom to refer all my difficulties to you, Sir, for no one is better able to resolve my doubts and to inform my ignorance. I have never been present at an examination of Christians. Consequently, I do not know the nature or the extent of the punishments usually meted out to them, nor the grounds for starting an investigation and how far it should be pressed. Nor am I at all sure whether any distinction should be made between them on the grounds of age, or if young people and adults should be treated alike; whether pardon ought to be granted to anyone retracting his beliefs, or if he has once professed Christianity, he shall gain nothing by renouncing it; and whether it is the mere name of Christian which is punishable, even if innocent of crime, or rather the crimes associated with the name.

For the moment this is the line I have taken with all persons brought before me on the charge of being Christians. I have asked them in person if they are Christians, and if they admit it, I repeat the question a second and third time, with a warning of the punishment awaiting them. If they persist, I order them to be led away for execution; for, whatever the nature of their admission, I am convinced that their stubbornness and unshakeable obstinacy ought not to go unpunished. There have been others similarly fanatical who are Roman citizens. I have entered them on the list of persons to be sent to Rome for trial.

Now that I have begun to deal with this problem, as so often happens, the charges are becoming more widespread and increasing in variety. An anonymous pamphlet has been circulated which contains the names of a number of accused person. Among these I considered that I should dismiss any who denied that they were or ever had been Christians when they had repeated after me a formula of invocation to the gods and had made offerings of wine and incense to your statue (which I had ordered to be brought into court for this purpose along with the images of the gods), and furthermore had reviled the name of Christ: none of which things, I understand, any genuine Christian can be induced to do.

Others, whose names were given to me by an informer, first admitted the charge and then denied it; they said that they had ceased to be Christians two or more years ago. They all did reverence to your statue and the images of the gods in the same way as the others, and reviled the name of Christ. They also declared that the sum total of their guilt or error amounted to no more than this: they had met regularly before dawn on a fixed day to chant verse alternately among themselves in honour of Christ as if to a god, and also to bind themselves by oath, not for any criminal purpose, but to abstain from theft, robbery and adultery, to commit no breach of trust and not to deny a deposit when called upon to restore it. After this ceremony it had been their custom to disperse and reassemble later to take food of an ordinary, harmless kind; but they had in fact given up this practice since my edict, issued on your instructions, which banned all political societies. This made me decide it was all the more necessary to extract the truth by torture from two slave-women, whom they call deaconesses. I found nothing but a degenerate sort of cult carried to extravagant lengths.

I have therefore postponed any further examination and hastened to consult you. The question seems to me to be worthy of your consideration, especially in view of the number of persons endangered; for a great many individuals of every age and class, both men and women, are being brought to trial, and this is likely to continue. It is not only the towns, but villages and rural districts too which are infected through contact with this wretched cult. I think though that it is still possible for it to be checked and directed to better ends, for there is no doubt that people have begun to throng to temples which had been almost entirely deserted for a long time; the sacred rites which had been allowed to lapse are being performed again, and flesh of sacrificial victims is on sale everywhere, though up till recently scarcely anyone could be found to buy it. It is easy to infer from this that a great many people could be reformed if they were given an opportunity to repent.

TRAJAN TO PLINY

You have followed the right course of procedure, my dear Pliny, in your examination of the cases of persons charged with being Christians, for it is impossible to lay down a general rule to a fixed formula. These people must not be hunted out; if they are brought before you and the charges against them is proved, they must be punished, but in the case of anyone who denies that he is a Christian, and makes it clear that he is not offering prayers to our gods, he is to be pardoned as a result of his repentance however suspect his past conduct may be. But pamphlets circulated anonymously must play no part in any accusation. They create the worst sort of precedent and are quite out of keeping with the spirit of our age.[10]

It was this kind of brutal, ruthless, and bloody political situation in which the church of the Acts of the Apostles found itself. But it was against this same brutal, ruthless, and bloody political situation that the church of the Acts of the Apostles fought and overcame when in A.D. 313, Constantine the Emperor of Rome, handed down the Edict of Milan granting religious tolerance to the Christians and, subsequently, in A.D. 325, proclaimed Christianity the religion of the Roman Empire.

RELIGIOUS, PHILOSOPHICAL, AND HERETICAL OPPOSITION TO THE CHURCH OF THE ACTS OF THE APOSTLES

It is clearly seen from the politico-historical situation of the church of the Acts of the Apostles that the Early Church's birth and movement in its world was not on flowery beds of ease. The situation was of such that Paul of the Acts was driven to say, after returning to Antioch on his first missionary journey, that ". . . through many tribulations we must enter the kingdom of God" (Acts 14:22). But there were other vigorous opponents which were to be faced by the church of the Acts of the Apostles; these were the religious and philosophical opponents and heresies which rose up before it and in its midst.

---

[10] Pliny, *Letters and Panegyricus*. Trans. by Betty Radice. Loeb Classical Library. No. 59. (Cambridge, Mass.: Harvard University Press, 1969), Bk. X Chps. XCVI-XCVII.

RELIGIOUS OPPOSITION

The church of the Acts of the Apostles was born in an environment of religious pluralism. The church found itself virtually surrounded by religious and philosophical groups which made its existence tenuous and its success questionable. But with grit and audacity, it plunged in to find a foothold and to make a place for itself. The first group which vigorously and relentlessly opposed the church of the Acts of the Apostles was the Pharisees. The Pharisees were a group of religious fanatics. In his article in *The Interpreter's Dictionary of the Bible*, Matthew Black describes the Pharisees as a group that, "...took its rise from among the ranks of . . . lay lawyers of the Greek period." They were a "...body of lay scribes that formed the core of the emerging Pharisees party...."[11] Religiously, the Pharisees had a highly developed angelology, a theology of the resurrection of the dead, and a theology of the spirit.[12]

Another group which provided opposition for the church of the Acts of the Apostles was the Sadducees. The Sadducees were a politico-religious sect which was oriented to the interests of the priestly aristocracy and the rich. They were extremely interested in maintaining a healthy political relationship with the Roman government. They opposed the Pharisees' belief of a resurrection of the body, of the existence of angels and spirits (*see*, Acts 23:8). They became a major opposition to the Apostles and the Early Church of the Acts because of their contrary teaching of the resurrection of the dead and the resurrection of Christ (cf., Acts 4:1-3; 5:17). Then of course,

---
[11] Matthew Black, "Pharisees," *Interpreter's Dictionary of the Bible*. George Arthur Buttrick, Ed. Vol. III. (Nashville: Abingdon Press, 1962). p. 776.
[12] Ibid., p. 778.

there were the Scribes, Chief Priests, and the Captain of the Jewish Temple. We come into frequent contact with these in the Acts of the Apostles.

To these groups should be added the mystery religions which came up out of Egypt and the Zoroastrian religion which came from the East. Also, the world in which the Early Church found itself was the scene of much superstition and belief in magic. A good example of this will be found in Acts 13 when Paul and Barnabas sailed to Cyprus and found at Paphos a Jewish false prophet by the name of Bar-Jesus who practiced in magic (Acts 13:4-12).

PHILOSOPHICAL OPPOSITION

The next set of opponents for the church of the Acts of the Apostles was those people who represented the philosophical systems of that day. The Stoics and Epicureans were prominent among the opposing philosophies faced by the Church. We really meet them in chapter 17 of Acts where Paul preaches his great sermon before them at the Areopagus on Mars Hill in Athens. The Stoics were religious in their philosophy. They believed in God, but their God was Nature; theirs was a natural religion, a natural theology. They had never heard of, nor could accept, a resurrection of Jesus from the dead. The Epicureans' philosophy was grounded in the belief that "pleasure" was the highest good. Therefore, they came to be known by the saying "eat, drink and be merry, for tomorrow we die."

A heresy which took the shape of a religious belief with a religious following which the church of the Acts of the Apostles faced was that of Gnosticism. Gnosticism was only one of the many heresies faced by the Early Church, but it possibly was the most powerful one faced by the church of the Acts. Gnosticism as a religion held that "knowledge" (the meaning of the word γνῶσις =*gnosis*) was the essence of life. This knowledge, which supposedly was revealed by God of the origin and destiny of mankind by means of the spiritual element in man, was the means of salvation. Gnostics believed that some men were constituted as having within them a seed or spark of Divine spiritual substance. They believed that the environment in which they lived, i.e., the world, was evil; they also believed that the body was evil, representing the prison house of the soul. They further believed that with "gnosis" (knowledge) and the rites associated with its spiritual element, the Gnostic would be delivered from his evil environment, the world and the body, and be rescued to return to his home in the Divine Being, the world of light. Jesus Christ for the Gnostics was the emissary of the supreme God who brought "gnosis" or knowledge to the world. Gnostics believed that Jesus, as a Divine being, neither assumed a human body nor died. They believed that Jesus temporarily inhabited a human body, or even made his appearance in a phantasmic (ghostly) human form.

Paul introduces us to the Gnostics in his letters to the Corinthians and Galatians. Walter Schmithals in his *Paul and the Gnostics* and *Gnosticism in Corinth* has called them Jewish Christian Gnostics. When Paul refers to the "spiritual man" of Corinth (πνευματικός=*pneumatikos*) who was supposed to possess Divine knowledge, he was referring to a Gnostic (cf., 1 Cor. 2:15). Those who were Gnostics at Corinth who had considered themselves to have full knowledge, which had been conveyed to them by the Divine Spirit, considered themselves wise. But they were not wise enough to prevent arguments and divisions which led to court fights among them. They considered themselves already to have arrived, which caused them to become arrogant (cf., 1 Cor. 4:6-21). Because they believed their bodies were evil and only served as the prison house of the soul, the seed, the Divine spark, they thought they could do anything they wished with their bodies without reprisal. So they ate and drank as they wished, often in excessive abundance. This is the reason for the controversy in 1 Corinthians 11 where Paul berated the Corinthians for getting drunk around the Lord's table while taking the Lord's Supper. Paul concluded, from reports he had heard, that there were some among the Corinthians whose morality had sunk lower than anything heard among the Gentiles. In the fifth chapter of 1 Corinthians, Paul remarks that a man was living with his father's wife (his step-mother?), and was arrogant about it. The heresy of Gnosticism at Corinth resulted in division, chaos, and abject immorality within the church. However, the church was able to overcome by the power and might of the Holy Spirit.

We are introduced to an example of the Gnostics in the Acts of the Apostles in the eighth chapter in the person of Simon Magus. A professional sorcerer, Simon Magus was known by his contemporaries as the Power of God and was called great. After ostensibly confessing Christianity, he was later rebuked by Peter for trying to acquire spiritual powers from the Apostles for money (this is called *simony*). It is believed that in the second and third centuries there arose a quasi-Christian sect which had a Gnostic orientation of which it is believed that Simon Magus was the founder. It is known that Gnosticism was recognized, taught and promoted by influential men such as Valentinus, Basilides, and Marcion. The Mandeans of Mesopotamia, the Manichees of Persia (third century), the Albigenses and Cathari of

France, Italy, and Germany were all groups which perpetuated the Gnostic religion.

There were other heretics and heresies faced by the church. Eusebius speaks of Menander the impostor. Eusebius says that Menander, who succeeded Simon Magus,

...exhibited himself in his conduct an instrument of diabolical wickedness, not inferior to the former. He also, was a Samaritan, and having made no less progress in his impostures than his master, revelled in still more arrogant pretensions to miracles; saying that he was in truth the Savior, once sent from the invisible worlds for the salvation of men; teaching also, that no one could overcome even the angels that formed the heavens in any way, than by being first initiated into the magic discipline imparted by him, and by the baptism conferred by him for this purpose. Of which, those who were deemed worthy would obtain perpetual immortality in this very life, being no more subject to death, but continuing here the same, would be exempt from old age, and be in fact immortal. . . . It was indeed, a diabolical artifice, by means of such impostors assuming the title of Christians, to evince so much zeal in defaming the great mystery of piety by magic arts, and to rend asunder by these means the doctrines of the church respecting the immortality of the soul, and the resurrection of the dead.[13]

Although Eusebius cites several other heretics and heresies in his *Ecclesiastical History*, one other comes to mind that seems very significant—that was the Ebionite Heresy. The Ebionites had a low opinion of the Christ, believed that he was not preexistent, i.e., that he was

---

[13]Eusebius Pamphilus, *The Ecclesiastical History*. Trans. by Christian Frederick Cruse. (Grand Rapids, Mich.: Baker Book House, 1955). Bk. III. Chap. XXVI.

not Eternal, and raised serious questions about the validity of certain Scriptures. Eusebius says:

> These...Ebionites...cherished low and mean opinions of Christ. For they considered him a plain and common man, and justified only by his advances in virtue, and that he was born of the Virgin Mary, by natural generation. With them the observance of the law was altogether necessary, as if they could not be saved, only by faith in Christ and a corresponding life. Others, however, besides these, but of the same name, indeed avoided the absurdity of the opinions maintained by the former, not denying that the Lord was born of the Virgin by the Holy Ghost, and yet in like manner, not acknowledging his pre-existence, though he was God, the word and wisdom, they turned aside into the same irreligion, as with the former they evinced great zeal to observe the ritual service of the law. These, indeed, thought on the one hand that all the epistles of the apostle ought to be rejected, calling him an apostate from the law, but on the other, only using the gospel according to the Hebrews, they esteem the others as of but little value. They also observe the Sabbath and other discipline of the Jews, just like them, but on the other hand, they also celebrate the Lord's days very much like us, in commemoration of his resurrection.[14]

Eusebius points to other heresies such as the Cerinthian and Nicolaitan heresies to show that the Early Church faced stiff competition from those who had perverted and corrupted the true teachings of the Christ and the Church. The Church was inevitably to face more and more heresies as it moved through the civilized world. The Church would confront the heresy of Arianism, a heresy which taught that Jesus Christ was not divine and eternal but was created by God the Father and was only

---

[14]Op. cit. Bk. III. Chap. XXVII.

the son of God because of the name God bestowed upon him in keeping with Jesus' abiding righteousness. The Church would confront Docetism, the tendency of some within The Faith to think that the humanity and suffering of Jesus Christ only seemed to be real but were not really so. They argued that somehow Christ miraculously escaped the shame of death due to Judas Iscariot or Simon of Cyrene changing places with him just before the crucifixion.

SUMMARY

So this was the world into which the church of the Acts of the Apostles was born and into which she moved to do battle for her Savior, proclaiming the Gospel of the Resurrection and the Kingdom of God. The church of the Acts of the Apostles would move into a political world which would not be a friend to grace. There would be trials and tribulations. Many would die of flames while tied to a stake, or would be beheaded at the guillotine, or would be torn apart by wild beasts, or would be made to kill one another while fighting as gladiators before screaming crowds in a coliseum, such as the one at Scythopolis (the Biblical Beth Shean). There were philosophical systems against which the Church had to contend. Religious pluralism which manifested itself in religious intolerance was to the Early Christian Church as it were a bed of prickling thorns, aggravating it; it were as a fiercely blowing wind testing those of The Faith of their ability to stand.

Then, there were heresies within the church threatening her with division and dissipation. There were

Roman authorities, secret agents, and informants whose purpose it was to seek out those of The Way and destroy them lest their movement become unmanageable. There were the Pharisees, Chief Priests, and Scribes who lurked around every corner waiting for an opportunity to catch and kill members of the church for violating ancient Hebrew laws. Every opportunity was used to carry members of the church before the Roman tribunal for some contrived violation of Roman law. This was the world in which the church of the Acts of the Apostles found herself and into which she moved as a mighty monolith, crushing, capturing, conquering, convicting, and convincing the world of her God-given power to overcome.

The Early Church of the Acts of the Apostles and the New Testament and the church of the Post-apostolic Era survived persecution after persecution. She survived the Decian Persecution of A.D. 250 and the Diocletian Persecution of A.D. 303. She demonstrated such an ability to survive persecution until Constantine proclaimed Christianity the religion of the Roman Empire in A.D. 325. The church continued her monolithic movement through the world as she conquered the lives of men like Augustine, converting them until the likes of Augustine became St. Augustine, Bishop of the Church at Hippo, Carthage, in North Africa, a writer of passionate conviction, writing that the City of Man (*Civitas Homo*) would soon become the City of God (*Civitas Dei*).

The church continued her monolithic movement as it survived the chances, changes, and challenges of the centuries. A survivor of the Dark Ages (Middle Ages), the church survived the Renaissance when, in the age of machines like the printing press, the Bible was slowly wrung from the sanctuary of the monastery and placed in the hands of common men. She survived the Reformation when Protestantism defiantly leaped from the womb of the Catholic Church and spawned an assortment of churches of various religious proclivities. The church survived American Slavery, the tampering of Holy Scripture to insure the enslavement of the ebony people of Africa. The church has survived the attempt of those who would cause it to be anything and everything but the church of the New Testament. The church has survived the age of industrialization; she has survived the age of aviation; the age of automation; the age of cybernation; and the age of computerization. Through every age, clime and time, the Church has survived and has thrived as a church of power.

My position is that Christians are a part of a movement, the Church, which is destined to survive all of the dangers and dares of this world. But it is also my position that the church is not only destined to survive, but to overcome the powers of evil in the world. The Acts of The Apostles provides the model, the blueprint, the chart and compass for such a venture. The question is whether we of today's church are willing to go back to the model, the blueprint, the map to see what to do and where to go from here. The world in which the church exists today is so very similar to the world into which the church of the Acts of Apostle was born and lived.

The nature of America today is of such that it has become a "nation with the soul of a church," as Sidney Mead has said. America as a nation is the end in itself for all of its citizens and demands blind devotion and patriotism whether right or wrong. The church has suffered persecution under this arrangement, e.g., Martin Luther King, Jr., was killed for the sake of the name of God, Jesus, and freedom. The world is so similar to that of the Early Church.

Religious pluralism, which in many cases manifests itself as religious intolerance, is a reality in our day. There is every religion conceivable in this country. As the church of the Acts of the Apostles faced heresies, so does the church of this day. There are sects and groups that hold that God is dead. There are those who are using the Christian Gospel and the Christian Church to foster their own cause and the accumulation of money. There are those who like Charles Manson, in the name of God and Jesus Christ, have announced that they have heard the voice of God declaring that the end of time is near, only to have that appointed time to come and pass without anything happening, thus leaving those who have followed to drift away in despair and hopelessness.

The society in which today's church finds herself has presented it with the challenge of crime, crime in the streets and crime in the suites, high-class crime, low-class crime. Dope is raping our youth of their vigor, robbing them of their hope. Sickness and disease are taking their toll on the sons of men of this society; living in this modern nation with the stress and strain of making a living is driving people completely mad. Our mental institutions are bursting at the seams. Our families are falling apart. The question is, "How will the church deal with this upside down society"?

It seems to me that the role of the church in this upside down society is modeled in the Acts of the Apostles. The question before us today is whether the church is willing to go back to the model and perform as it was designed by the drawer of the plan, Jesus Christ the Son of God.

Chapter II

THE CENTER OF POWER FOR THE CHURCH: THE MANDATE TO WITNESS

The center of power for the church of the Acts of the Apostles was clearly that of witnessing. There is no clearer manifestation of this than that of the Early Church receiving power by means of witnessing to the resurrection of the Christ. Witnessing in the name of Jesus is at the center of the story of the church in Acts. Power for the church of the Acts of the Apostles was not to be acquired by means of "sound doctrine" or proper ecclesiastical structure as would be the case of the church of the Pastoral Epistles of a much later time. It would come from witnessing to the name of Jesus.

Luke opens the Acts of the Apostles by addressing his work to Theophilus, the one to whom the book was written. His reference to the "first book" (Acts 1:1) obviously is in reference to the Gospel of Luke, his story of the life and works of Jesus. Luke says:

> In the first book...I have dealt with all that Jesus began to do and teach, until the day when he was taken up, after he had given commandment through the Holy Spirit to the apostles whom he had chosen. (Acts 1:1-2 RSV)

Then in verse three of the first chapter, Luke harks back to Jesus' appearance before the disciples (Luke 24:36-40) where Jesus, after the disciples had gathered together in Jerusalem, came and stood in their midst and said to them, "Why are you troubled, and why do questionings rise in your hearts? See my hands and my feet that it is I myself: handle me, and see; for a spirit has not flesh and bones as you see that I have." Then in the fourth verse of the first chapter of Acts, Luke refers again to something he has already said in the Gospel Story where Jesus charged the disciples to stay in Jerusalem and wait for the promise of the Father. He says, "...for John baptized with water, but before many days you shall be baptized with the Holy Spirit."

It is to be noted that to assure the disciples of the authenticity of the appearance of Jesus on the Easter side of the grave, Luke refers to his experience of breaking bread with them both while at the village of Emmaus and when he met with them in Jerusalem before his ascension. In the fourth verse, the phrase "while staying with them," can mean both "while staying" and "while eating." It was while staying with them and while eating with the disciples in both Emmaus and Jerusalem, that the disciples knew Jesus was the risen Savior. In Luke 24, it was while two disciples were walking dejectedly on their way to the village of Emmaus that Jesus drew near to them and walked with them on the way. But the record states that, "...their eyes were kept from recognizing him" (or "their eyes were beholden," KJV). But in Luke 24:28ff., when they drew near to the village, they constrained Jesus to stay with them for, they said, "...it is toward evening and the day is far spent." So Jesus went in to the village and stayed with them. Then they sat down at the table and the record is that, "...he took...bread and blessed, and broke it, and gave it to them. And their eyes were opened and they recognized him." And again, in that same chapter (Luke 24), after showing the disciples His hands and feet, Jesus again asked for something to eat (v. 41). They gave Him a piece of broiled fish and He ate it before them.

In the Gospel of John (John 21:9-14), Jesus is also recorded as revealing Himself to His disciples through the breaking of bread. The point here is that the disciples did not know the resurrected Savior until the breaking of the bread over the table of fellowship with Him. There is tremendous theological significance here because only in the breaking of the bread with His disciples is the identity of Jesus as the resurrected Savior authenticated. Only in this act is Jesus known to His disciples. The deeper meaning implied here is that the knowledge of Jesus is revealed to the disciples of the Church through their participation in the bread and wine of the Holy Sacrament. The church believed Jesus commissioned believers to observe this ritual as a sacred meal. It ultimately became an ordinance of the church. Paul would say in 1 Corinthians 10:16, "The cup of blessing which we bless, is it not a participation in the blood of Christ? The bread which we break, is it not a participation in the body of Christ?" It follows then, that the disciples to whom Jesus revealed Himself could only execute His master plan for the Church and carry out His divine orders if they knew Him; and they would know Him through the breaking of the bread.

It follows, therefore, that "the center of power of the church" today comes when it knows Jesus as the resurrected Savior. The church comes to know the Master in the breaking of the bread, in the observance of the Lord's Supper. This knowledge of the Christ is the beginning of power. This then calls for a reassessment of the meaning of the Lord's Supper as it is observed in our churches on the First Sunday morning (or whenever it is observed). For the observance of the Lord's Supper, the participation in the bread, the body of Christ, and the wine, the blood of Christ, is not necessarily "the medicine of immortality" as it was said by Ignatius. It is not a stroke of magic to assure us eternal life, nor a good luck piece to protect us from sickness and suffering in this life. It is an experience with Christ, coming to know Him and committing ourselves to Him and to the work of witnessing to His name that His Kingdom might come on earth as it is in heaven.

So Luke says that, ". . .while staying with them [or, 'while eating with them'], he charged them not to depart from Jerusalem, but to wait for the promise of the Father, which, he said, "you heard from me, for John baptized with water, but before many days you shall be baptized with the Holy Spirit" (Acts 1:4f).

Verse six in this first chapter of Acts brings us to a crucial point in the passage. When they had come together, the disciples asked Jesus. "Lord, will you at this time restore the kingdom to Israel?" Now, the disciples asked the right question. It was a moral, ethical, religious, and political question. In their own mind, the moral, ethical, religious, and political situation in Palestine was wrong; and they were asking the Lord, on the eve of his ascension back to Glory, whether this was the time when he would set things right. Was this the time to establish the right order by God? Is this the eschatological end of time?

The disciples' question was one which rose up out of great and terrible frustration and weariness of soul. For as we have cited in the first lecture, the times in which the church of the Acts of the Apostles was born and found its existence were horrible, indeed. It was as Shakespeare once said in his play, *Hamlet*, "The times are out of joint." The times were out of joint for the disciples and the Early Church. The disciples wanted to know if the Lord was ready to "set them right." The Roman government, in collusion with the Sacerdotal Hierarchy of the Jewish Temple, had killed Jesus at Calvary and had given Him a criminal's death. The Neronian persecution had already taken its toll on the church. Christians were being falsely charged, killed, maimed, burned at the stakes, fed to dogs and wild animals, and the Holy Land was under the heavy and sacrilegious burden of Roman taxation. Families were being destroyed; robbery, trickery, and deceit were stalking the land unafraid. The demons of disease were plaguing the bodies of humanity, and mental illness was rending asunder the minds of the people. In the powers of man, there seemed to be no remedy for it all. Religion was flourishing but righteousness was fading. Self-made saviors were rising up in every quarter, claiming to be deliverers, confusing the minds of the people and leading many astray. There seemed to be a thirst for magic and superstition which held captive the spirits of man. So in the disciples' mind, and rightly so, everything was bad, nothing was good. The times were all wrong, and they wanted to know if the Lord was now ready to set things right; if He was now ready to usher in the eschatological parousia; if He was ready to establish a kingdom, the reign of God as it was during the time of David in ancient Israel. This was the disciples' question.

But this was not only the disciples' question to the risen Lord on Mt. Olivet's hill; it is our question now, in our day and time. We want to know if God is ready to set right a world and a nation gone wrong. There is no question of whether things are wrong. In our country, unemployment for Black adults rose to a staggering rate of about 12%, and Black teenagers topped out at 40%. There is little energy generated in America toward providing jobs for these people. While visiting Washington, D.C., in the early 1980's, to lobby for the Humphrey-Hawkins full employment bill, we discovered that some legislators such as Senator Howard Baker of Tennessee were more concerned with how much inflation this bill would create rather than the number of jobs it would provide for the unemployed. In the face of such quibbling and protracted debate, social programs were being cut by the government, and middle and upper-class Whites were launching a tax revolt (such as Proposition 13 in California).

And what is the result of high unemployment among Black and poor people? I will tell you! The result is thousands of Black and poor youth who are idle; and being idle, with nothing in their pockets, they commit crimes to survive. They join gangs of their peers and set out to destroy the society which seems to be no friend to them. They turn to drugs which are readily supplied to them by the Mafia, the FBI, and the CIA. They end up in a prison system where they find more provision for them by the government than they did while they were in civilian life, where they could not find a job. Further, high unemployment among Black and poor people has resulted in a spiraling increase in mental strain and sickness: More Black people today are committing suicide than ever before. Unemployment is tearing the Black family apart. Tension is growing stronger and stronger, drawing the Black man who cannot find a decent job, or cannot find a job at all, farther away from his wife who has always been able to find both a job and a place in this society.

Our question today is much like that of the disciples on Mt. Olivet. When we pastors sit in our studies pondering deeply the situation about us, we are almost driven to despair because of the hell and chaos that rage about us. It comes from the wickedness of unwillingness in government, crime which is stalking the streets unafraid, and more than this, the worry we have over our churches. When we think about all this, our question becomes the disciples' question: "Lord, will you at this time restore the kingdom to Israel?"

Notice how the disciples styled the question. They wanted to know if the Lord is now ready to restore the kingdom to Israel. They wanted to know if the Lord was ready to do it. They felt, in their despair and frustration, that there was nothing they could do; it was out of their hands. I think this is our feeling today! Many of us in the church feel there is nothing we can do; it is out of our hands. Many people and clergy alike are saying like weeping Jeremiah in the eighth chapter of that passionate and prophetic Old Testament book, "The harvest is past, the summer is ended, and we are not saved" (Jeremiah 8:20).

The Martin Luther King Jr. Era came, and there beamed the gilded rays of promise and hope for a better day for Black people in this nation. But Martin has been here and gone, and things still are no better. Our people are not yet saved! Even some of those who as preachers walked and worked with Martin during his more than thirteen years of ministry to this world, walk no longer among those of us who are couriers of the Gospel of Jesus Christ. Some of the preachers of Martin's movement, preachers who worked and hoped for the better and utopian day for Black people, are no longer preaching the Gospel, but have sought to make their contribution in other areas of life. There is a deep and terrifying feeling of frustration and despair among the people. Those of us who remain in the church feel a sense of helplessness; the church is so helplessly divided with denominations here and denominations there, denominations which are totally separated from one another with an agenda all their own. Churches are in competition with one another and congregations are in competition with themselves.

Pastors are preoccupied with tricky trustees and deceitful deacons, unruly groups, and quarrels within the church. All of this covers our sky with clouds of gloom and despair, and we draw the conclusion that the situation is out of our hands. So, we want to know if God, the Lord, is now ready to set things right, is he now ready to establish a new kingdom among the sons of men? This is what the disciples wanted to know. It is our question as well!

They were asking the right question, but with the wrong motive. Listen to the question again: "Lord will you at this time restore the kingdom to Israel?" The question, though rightly intended, had the wrong motive. The disciples wanted the Lord to restore the situation to what it was during the days of the Davidic Kingdom, when David-Zion was the shrine of the Holy Land of the Israelites; when there was peace in the land and every man sat under his own vine and fig tree; when the Hebrews had a homeland of their own. This was what they wanted. It was a selfish request; they wanted a kingdom all their own. They asked the right question, but with the wrong motive.

I think Black people must be careful how we ask God to set things right in this world today. It could be that we would ask the right question with the wrong motive. In asking God to set things right, we may be asking Him to establish a kingdom dominated by Black people. This could very well be what we want for ourselves rather than what God wants for us. I conclude that it is dangerous for any people to aspire to set up a nation, a kingdom, exclusively for themselves. For in doing so, they are really saying that they are the favorites of God while other people are wrong. This is a dangerous request.

One hundred and forty-five years before Jesus came into the world, the Pharisees—known as the "separated ones," sought to organize a pure Jewish religion and nation. They were so dogmatic that even when Jesus, the Son of God, came into the world, they did all they could to conspire to kill the Lord because he was not like them. White people who settled America made this request of God. They thought God gave them a divine mandate, a "manifest destiny," to enslave Black people from Africa and to kill the indigenous Indians of America. So they pursued it without any moral or religious restraint, in order to settle a country for themselves.

Hitler's Germany wanted to establish a nation for itself, a nation of pure Teutonic, Germanic stock. In doing so, they felt no qualms about killing six million Jews at Dachau, Auschwitz, and other German prison camps where ovens were made hot and ready. It is dangerous to ask God to establish a kingdom exclusively for a particular people. To do so can plunge even the church into the demonic imbroglio of what Paul Tillich called "authoritarianism." Therefore, I have drawn the conclusion that it is not the right direction in which Black people should go when we talk about a Black nation, like the Black Muslims, or a Black Christian Nationalism as espoused by Albert Cleage, or a Black church, especially when they talk about them exclusively and absolutely. It could be that in setting up such a situation, we would do so at the expense of others and against the will of God.

So, the disciples on the Mount of Olives were asking Jesus the right question but with the wrong motive. But then, there is something positive to be said about a people asking the right question even though it is with the wrong motive. The question the disciples asked Jesus, even though it was with the wrong motive, reflected the fact that they yet had in their mind the vision of a coming kingdom that Jesus had spoken about in the early days of his preaching ministry. This capacity to have the vision of God in their mind—the vision of a new age, the reign of God on earth as it is in heaven—was in the disciples' favor. For God has always been able to use men who had the capacity to catch His vision.

The eighth century prophets of the Old Testament were men who effected social change because they were men of vision. Isaiah was a prophet who envisioned a time when a child would be born and a son would be given:

". . .and the government will be upon his shoulder, and his name will be called Wonderful Counselor, Mighty God, Everlasting Father, Prince of Peace. Of the increase of his government and of peace there will be no end, upon the throne of David, and over his kingdom, to establish it, and to uphold it with justice and with righteousness from this time forth and for evermore. . . ." (Isaiah 9:6f)

He envisioned a time when men would beat their swords into plowshares and study war no more (Isaiah 2:4). Daniel envisioned a time of the coming of the "Ancient of Days" who would establish a kingdom that would be everlasting and would not pass away (Daniel 7:13f). John of the Revelation envisioned a time when ". . .the kingdoms of this world are become the kingdoms of our Lord, and of his Christ; and he shall reign for ever and ever (Revelation 11:15 KJV).

God could use Martin Luther King, Jr. to break down the walls of segregation because he had the vision of God that one day White men and Black men would sit down together at the table of brotherhood. Martin's vision was so powerfully vivid that he, like all other prophets before him, would be willing to die for it. So there was something positive about the disciples' question to Jesus regarding the establishment of His kingdom; it reflected their vision of a better world, a vision for which eventually, they were willing to die. It was these kind of men whom Jesus was able to use and to empower with the Holy Spirit to change the world.

So once the disciples had asked the Lord the crucial question, whether it was time for Him to restore the kingdom to Israel, the Lord responded with a startling proposition. He responded by saying, "It is not for you to know the times or seasons which the Father has put in His own authority" (Acts 1:7 NKJV). Jesus was harking back to what He had said in the Gospels (Matthew 24:36 and Mark 13:32), "But of that day and hour knoweth no man, no, not the angels of heaven. . . but my Father only" (Matthew 24:36 KJV). In other words, Jesus was saying to the disciples of the church of the Acts of the Apostles—he was really giving them an injunction against asking such questions—"It was not for them to know. . .it was not their concern."[15] Jesus was saying that it was not their business to spend time pondering when the historical affairs of men would come to an end, or when God would choose to break into time to manifest Himself in divine activity; the times of such activity the Father has fixed by His own authority. It is not for you to know!

It is interesting to note that after Jesus set this injunction before the disciples of the Early Church, they never raised the question again. But this is more than can be said for religious fanatics of our age. Some segments of the Christian church have not dealt so well with Jesus' injunction. They not only have brought history around

---

[15] F. F. Bruce, *The Acts of the Apostles*. (Grand Rapids, Mich.: William B. Eerdmans Publishing Company, 1970), p. 70.

full circle to ask the disciples' question, they have sought to assume the role of God and to answer the question as well. In 1844, the Adventists, known also as the Seventh-Day Adventists, took the liberty to announce the second coming of Jesus Christ and, thus, the end of the world. Likewise, C. T. Russell of the Jehovah's Witnesses, violated the injunction of Jesus on the Mount of Olives and announced the coming of the end of the world; and, he intimated that no one would be saved but the "elect of Jehovah" who would be the sole members of the Messianic Kingdom.

The sadness about the Seventh-Day Adventists and the Jehovah's Witnesses is that their prophecies came to nought. They did not realize it was not for them to know the times or seasons fixed by the Father in His authority. This will be the end result of anyone or any movement which takes into their hands the authority of God to pronounce judgment about the end of time. This is reserved for God alone.

Jesus moves on to quickly deal with the disciples' question in verse six. He does not answer their question, He corrects it. He says, "you ask me whether I am now ready to restore the kingdom. Well, I am going to establish a kingdom; I am going to set things right. But I am not going to do it myself. You are going to do it for me. I am going to give you a plan, a blueprint; and if you follow the plan, the blueprint, you will turn the world upside down and rightside up. 'But ye shall receive power, after that the Holy Ghost is come upon you'" (Acts 1:8a KJV). This is the first phase of the plan. Jesus promises to give power to the disciples, the church of the Acts of the Apostles.

In Matthew 28:18, Jesus said that "all power is given unto me in heaven and in earth" (the word used here is ἐξουσία=*exousia*, which also is translated "power" or "authority"); then He gives the disciples the Great Commission and sends them into all the world. But here in the Acts, Jesus promises to give the disciples not only a great commission but power—power to perform miracles, power to heal sicknesses, power to cast out demons, power to change the world from wrong to right. The word used for "power" is δύναμιν=*dunamin*, the same word that is used for dynamite. Luke uses this same word when he refers to the incident when Jesus returns from his testing with the devil in the wilderness. He says, ". . .Jesus returned in the power [*dunamei*] of the Spirit into Galilee. . ." (Luke 4:14). Paul the Apostle uses the same word when he says, "For I am not ashamed of the gospel of Christ: for it is the power [*dunamis*] of God unto salvation to every one that believeth. . ." (Romans 1:16 KJV). This power, Jesus said, would be given to the disciples of the church of the Acts of the Apostles when the Holy Spirit comes upon them (the same word used here is used when the angel Gabriel announces to Mary that the Holy Spirit would come upon her and she would conceive and bear a son). The power of the Holy Spirit would come upon the disciples through the medium of prayer. When they gathered in the Upper Room and engaged themselves in prayer, the Holy Spirit would come upon them in power. The Holy Spirit would empower the disciples to overcome sickness, sin, and wickedness. If they waited in prayer for the coming of the Holy Spirit, God would give them power to change the world. Right would no longer be on the scaffold and wrong would no longer be on the throne. The empowerment of the Holy Spirit would come through the medium of prayer. This was the first phase of Jesus' plan for the church of the Acts of the Apostles.

The second phase of the plan for the establishment of His Kingdom in the world was given to the disciples when the Lord said, "...and ye shall be witnesses unto me both in Jerusalem, and in all Judea, and in Samaria and unto the uttermost part of the earth" (Acts 1:8). By this means, accompanied by the power of the Holy Spirit, the disciples and the church of the Acts of the Apostles would change the world and make it a better place in which people could live. Notice what Jesus says, "ye shall be witnesses." He does not say that "you may elect" to be witnesses; he says "if you want to be my disciples and if you want to change the world to be a better place for humanity, *ye shall* be witnesses unto me." It is a mandate to witness! ... not in their own name, but in the name of Jesus Christ. It is an order coming from the Chief Commander of the Christian Army that when they fight, they must do so in His name. I say "Christian Army" advisedly, because the Lord was not preparing to send out a society of socialites, but an army of soldiers armed in the power of the Spirit. No! The Christian church is not a society of socialites; it is an army. It is not a museum; it is a movement for righteousness. So when we read the Acts of the Apostles, we are not reading bed-time stories to help us sleep more soundly, as James D. Smart says in *The Silence of the Bible in the Church*, we are reading marching orders for an army. Jesus said to the disciples, "And ye shall be witnesses unto me both in Jerusalem, and in all Judea, and in Samaria, and unto the uttermost part of the earth" (Acts 1:8b).

Another point of extreme significance in Jesus' plan for His church is that he says the disciples shall be *witnesses*. The emphasis is placed on the word "witnesses" because it meant more than preaching and testifying; it meant that and more. It meant suffering for the name of

Jesus Christ. The word used is μάρτυρες =*martures*, which comes from "μάρτυροσ =*marturos*." The word means "one who suffers" or "to suffer," even unto death for the sake of Christ. So Jesus really was saying to the disciples that if they wanted to see a better world about them, they must witness to His name even to the point of suffering and dying for the sake of His name.

The disciples were willing, then, to suffer punishment and abuse for the name sake of the Christ. When Peter and John were brought before the Sanhedrin Council for healing the lame man who laid at the Gate called Beautiful, when they were tried, beaten and released, Luke says in Acts 5:41, "Then they left the presence of the council, rejoicing that they were counted worthy to suffer dishonor *for the name*" (emphasis mine). Stephen was stoned to death and gladly gave up his life because of his witness to the name of Christ. Imprisonment awaited Peter at Jerusalem as well as Paul later at Philippi because of their unshakable witness to the Name of Jesus. Jesus was saying to the disciples at the Mount of Olives that if they wanted to be a power-centered church, they must witness to His name and be willing to suffer and die for His name. This was His plan for the church.

So when Jesus got ready to send His disciples out into a wicked and warped world, the world of the Roman Empire, their efforts to change that world to become a place of righteousness and peace was only accompanied by a double-barreled weapon of "prayer" and a "witness." But that "prayer" and "witness" would also be accompanied by power in the Holy Spirit. This was His plan; but by this plan, the Early Church would turn the world upside down.

CONCLUSION

My proposition is that Jesus's plan for a power-centered church is still viable and functional. For the church to be power centered, she must exercise prayer and witnessing. If the church prays and witnesses, according to the plan which Jesus left on record, she is assured to receive power to change the world, power in the Holy Spirit. If the church is failing today, it is not because the plan is faulty; it is because there has been little fealty to the plan. The contemporary church has little power because she has lost the vision of the kingdom of God on earth as it is in heaven. She has lost sight of the fact that the church is an army of Christian soldiers engaged in a movement for righteousness, marching under orders from Jesus who is her Commander. The contemporary church has little power because she has taken on the form of a museum where people come to look at each other to see how well each is dressed. The contemporary church has little power because she has taken on the form of a society of socialites more concerned with its situation than its vocation in the kingdom. The church is more concerned with her bank account than she is with whether its members have settled **The Old Account**. However, while the church today has this museum mentality and this socialite sensation, the world about her is crumbling. The church today has not taken seriously Jesus' plan of prayer and witnessing; and, as a result, she does not have the power that is manifested in the Holy Spirit.

The church today is engaged in a lot of things, but she is not engaged in prayer and witnessing. We preach on Sunday morning at the 11 o'clock A.M. worship service in the comfort of a modern sanctuary; we have singing programs on Sunday nights; we have week-long revivals where nobody is saved. We have pastors' anniversaries; we have building fund campaigns to build bigger and more beautiful buildings; we go to conventions and congresses, but we don't have the power of the Holy Spirit that comes through prayer and witnessing. I dare say that the most poorly attended service we have in our churches is the prayer meeting, and some churches do not have prayer meeting because of poor attendance. There is little need to mention that the church does not have programs where it goes out into the world to witness to the name of Jesus. Yes! We do a lot of church work but not much work of the church. There is very little prayer and witnessing which result in a changed world through the power of the Holy Spirit. The contemporary church has little power, not because it has no plan from God, but because it has not followed the plan. It is my position here that in light of the situation facing our world, the church must turn back to the plan which Jesus left on record and become a praying and witnessing church, or she should renounce her name as the Church of Jesus Christ, throw away the Bible and call herself something else, board up its doors and windows and go out of business.

If the contemporary church is to be power-centered, she has a plan which calls for prayer and witnessing. Through the faithful execution of this plan, the church will receive redemptive power through the Holy Spirit. To the surprise of the church, she will discover that the plan will work. Jesus did not send His disciples into the world without a plan. He guaranteed that if they followed the plan, they would change the world. So it was that when Peter and John went up to the Temple at the hour of prayer, they saw a cripple man who had lain at the Gate called Beautiful, all they had was prayer on their mind and in their hearts and a testimony about Jesus on their lips. They looked at that man and said, "Silver and gold have I none; but such as I have give I thee: In the name of Jesus Christ of Nazareth rise up and walk" (Acts 3:6). Luke says that Peter took the man by the right hand and raised him up and immediately the man's feet and ankles became strong. "And he leaping up stood, and walked, and entered with them into the temple, walking, and leaping, and praising God." In the eighth chapter of Acts, Philip went down to Samaria, a nation bitter with strife and torn by hatred; racial prejudice for the Jews ran oceans deep in Samaria. But it was to Samaria that Philip was sent to preach in the name of Jesus Christ. There were people with unclean spirits in Samaria, people paralyzed and lame; all Philip had with him was a witness about Jesus. The Bible says that after Philip preached Jesus in Samaria, ". . .there was great joy in that city." And Simon Peter, a Jew himself, went down to Samaria and associated with the Samaritans, and prayed for them that they might receive the Holy Spirit. When he prayed and laid hands on them, they received the Holy Spirit.

All through the twenty-eight chapters of the Acts of the Apostles, the church moved like a mighty monolith, walking over wickedness, raising up the wrecked and the wretched, rising above unrighteousness, crushing corruption, crumbling nations and kingdoms in its path; all it had was a prayer and a witness that gave it power in the Holy Spirit. But the story of the magnificent unfolding drama of the Early Church does not end with the twenty-eighth chapter of the Book of Acts, for the church which Jesus founded on the Mount of Olives side of the grave with eleven disciples who had a vision of a better world, kept marching on. The church marched through Asia Minor. She marched through the Roman Empire till she came to the mighty city of Rome; she came, she saw, and she conquered the mighty city of Rome. But she did not stop there! The church marched over the altitudinous Alps and the jagged snowcapped mountains of France and through the rolling hills and clover-laden vales of Germany and into the fog-shrouded isles of Great Britain. She marched through the dark ages, through the Renaissance, the Reformation, and on to this day. All the church has had as weapons has been "prayer" and "witnessing." She did not have ammunition and guns; all she had was prayer and witnessing.

I believe Jesus' plan yet works if it is tried. I read a story in the newspaper some time ago about a woman who was being robbed in a store in Chattanooga, Tennessee. The robber had knocked the woman to the floor and placed a knife at her throat. Suddenly she looked the robber in his eyes and said, "In the name of Jesus Christ, I command that you leave me alone." The story said that the man froze and could not move. He was apprehended by police and arrested, tried by a court, and put in prison. But he said he could never forget what that woman said to him, her witness to the name of Jesus. He wrote the woman and told her that since that day he had never been the same. He had given his life to Jesus, and his life was not the same. The essence of that story is that criminals and culture itself can be changed by witnessing in the name of Jesus. I believe the church today must be power-centered through its prayer and witness to the name of Jesus the Christ. When this happens, drug addicts will be cured; prostitutes will come off the streets; prodigal sons will come home from the far country; sicknesses will be healed, and sins will be forgiven.

Jesus said to His disciples when they asked if He was ready to restore the kingdom to Israel:

> It is not for you to know the times or the seasons, which the Father hath put in his own power. But ye shall receive power, after that the Holy Ghost is come upon you: and ye shall be witnesses unto me both in Jerusalem, and in all Judea, and Samaria, and unto the uttermost part of the earth. (Acts 1:7-8)

Chapter III

POWER AS THE FOUNDATION OF THE CHURCH

How a thing gets started has all to do with how it does after it starts. If it gets off to a good beginning, chances are it will do well during its operation. How well a foundation is laid has all to do with the strength of the building which is to be built upon it. The church of the Acts of the Apostles was like a mighty rocket launched from the hillside of Mount of Olives. It needed a mighty force of power to be launched; but once it was launched, it would be propelled by the force and power of its launching. The church of the Acts of the Apostles was like a mighty tower built on a sure and unshakeable foundation. The tornadic winds of trials and tribulations would fiercely blow, but the church would stand fast. This is the church of the Acts of the Apostles, a church which had power as its foundation.

If there is anything that is clear about the Acts of the Apostles, it is its disclosure of the beginnings of the Church of Jesus Christ as having a "center of power." This message from Luke is clear from the beginning of the book. The first two chapters are the launching pad for the church; and, there is no question that the church had beginnings with a center of power. Our purpose in these lectures is to reexamine the Book of Acts to see how the

Early Church acquired its power and hopefully to suggest ways today's church might acquire the same. My basic thesis in this chapter is that the contemporary church must be built on a foundation of power and propelled through history by power. Power must be the essence of her being.

Beginnings are important. The beginning of the power-centered church of the Acts of the Apostles is carefully laid out. Luke takes two chapters to acquaint us with the laying of the foundation of a church that was soon to be empowered by the Holy Spirit. These are the two chapters at which we will look—Acts 1:12-2:47. Once Jesus had given his disciples his general plan and blueprint for the new kingdom which the church was to establish, he ascended back to heaven. While he ascended into the heavens and the disciples looked in bewilderment at his departure, two men in white apparel stood by them saying that The Lord would return in the same manner in which they saw him leave. This is obviously Luke's way of reminding the reader of the Parousia, the Second Coming of Jesus at the *eschaton*.

The disciples returned from the Mount of Olives to Jerusalem and to the Upper Room where they were staying. Immediately, Luke called the names of the disciples who had gathered in the Upper Room along with Mary, the mother of Jesus, the brothers of Jesus, and certain women. He names Peter and John and James and Andrew, Philip and Thomas, Bartholomew and Matthew, James the son of Alphaeus, Simon the Zealot, and Judas the son of James. They are eleven in number. Judas Iscariot is missing. Luke's purpose for naming the disciples is to point out that Judas, who was one of the twelve, was missing. Now, these eleven disciples, and the others who made up the 120 who were in the Upper Room, knew there was something they had to do in order to restore the number of disciples to its former composition, the number twelve. They knew there was something which had to be done to their organizational structure before the Holy Spirit could come upon them with power. Their organizational structure was not right to receive the Holy Spirit. The number eleven was incomplete. The number twelve was significant for the church; it represented the entire church, as it represented the entire group of disciples. As many as ten times, the Gospel of Mark refers to the disciples as "the twelve." In Mark 3:14, it says, "And he appointed twelve, to be with him, and to be sent out to preach and have authority to cast out demons." In Mark 4:10, reference is made to "the twelve." Mark 6:7, says, "And he called to him the twelve, and began to send them out two by two...." In Mark 9:35 and 10:32, Jesus talked with "the twelve" as he went toward Jerusalem. In Mark 11:11, Jesus goes out to Bethany with "the twelve." Then in Mark 14:10, as is the rest of the references in Mark's Gospel, reference to "the twelve" is in relation to Judas. Mark 14:10, says, "Then Judas Iscariot, who was one of *the twelve*, went to the chief priests in order to betray him to them." In Mark 14:17, Jesus sits down at the table with "the twelve" and speaks of one of the disciples who is to betray him; when the question is raised by each of the disciples, "Is it I who will betray you?" Jesus says, "It is one of *the twelve*, one who is dipping bread in the same dish with me." Finally, in Mark 14:43, the record says that while Jesus was in the Garden of Gethsemane praying, "Judas came, *one of the twelve*," to betray his Lord (emphases mine). So the eleven were faced with the awesome task of restoring the disciples to their rightful composition, the number twelve. They knew they had to do this before the Holy Spirit could come. They knew they had to get the structure of the church right before strength could come.

This is an extremely significant point to ponder if today's church is to be power-centered. It needs to be sure its leadership is rightly established and rightly recognized. Then and only then can the Holy Spirit come and bestow upon the church the endowments of power. I pastored a church which had its beginnings altogether different from that which is called for in the plan which is laid before us in the Acts of the Apostles. Ever since its inception in 1920, it experienced an absence of power. The history of the beginnings of Westwood Baptist Church states that the congregation was formed first without the establishment or recognition of the leadership of a pastor. History discloses that there was a group of people who wanted to have a church of their own; so they met from house to house, and finally organized themselves into a church which was called "Westwood." Then someone was called to do the preaching.[16] This was not the way the church of the Acts of the Apostles did it. Those 120 people who gathered in the Upper Room saw to it that they first established the leadership of the church. Whenever you chose to do it in a way contrary to God's plan, you are bound to have trouble and you are bound not to be a power-centered church. The church will not have power in the world without, because it would have dissipated itself in power struggles within.

The eleven disciples were determined to get themselves together in preparation for the coming of the power of the Holy Spirit. They needed direction for what to do to resolve the problem. What did they do? They prayed! Acts 1:14 says, "All these [referring to the eleven and the

---

[16]The author is no longer pastor of Westwood Church. He is presently pastor of Zion Hill First African Baptist Church in Nashville, Tennessee.

others who made up the 120] with one accord devoted themselves to prayer...." Prayer became the medium by which the disciples solved the problem of the replacement of Judas and the restoration of the leadership of the church to its composition of twelve disciples. But prayer was not only the medium by which the church solved this problem, it was the medium by which they solved every problem and situation they faced. Prayer, in the church of the Acts of the Apostles became the theological necessity for every move it made.

Prayer became a key factor in making the church of the Acts of the Apostles power-centered. The church learned the importance of prayer from its Master and had been charged by Him to develop a life of prayer, to wait (in prayer) on the coming of the Holy Spirit, and to pray for guidance. They remembered how their Master prayed in his lifetime. Luke records at least seven times when Jesus prayed at crucial moments in his life: At his baptism, he prayed (Luke 3:21f); after he had performed many miracles, he prayed (Luke 5:16); just before choosing his twelve disciples, he prayed (Luke 6:12); just before Peter made his great confession at Caesarea Philippi, Jesus was praying (Luke 9:18); when he went up to the Mount of Transfiguration, Jesus prayed (Luke 9:28). It was when Jesus was praying that his disciples came to him and asked, "Lord, teach us to pray, as John taught his disciples" (Luke 11:1). In the Garden of Gethsemane, Jesus prayed (Luke 22:41). So the church learned the importance of steadfastness in prayer from her Master; and in this situation of replacing Judas, the church sought God's guidance in prayer; she prayed when the Holy Spirit came; she prayed when the Lord brought victory to the church (Acts 5:41); she prayed when the church got in trouble (Acts 12:5; 16:25). The Early Church came to be power-centered, because it learned the importance of steadfastness in prayer.

I said in the previous chapter that the weakest part of the program of today's church is its prayer meeting. I believe the church is not strong in the world, especially the Black church, because it is weak in prayer. No church is able to stand up for righteousness in the world if it is not able to bow down in prayer before God. No church knows how to solve the problems within as well as without, unless it is in communion with the One who has the answer to every question and the solution to every problem *viz.*, God.

The Bible says that the eleven disciples and the rest of the 120 people in that Upper Room, devoted themselves to, or continued steadfastly in, prayer. Through prayer, the Holy Spirit disclosed what they had to do to get themselves together. They first had to deal with the tragedy of Judas. Now this was to the credit of the disciples in the Upper Room; for they, through the guidance of the Holy Spirit, saw that they had to deal with one of the darkest chapters in their history. They had to talk about the betrayal of Judas, i.e. Judas' betrayal of the Lord. For the most part, most churches today will not deal with the dark chapters in their history; they want to lay to rest, sweep under the rug, the years of storms and strife. I would dare say that the history of most churches is one which does not tell of her failures and that of her pastors and members. When I first read the history of Westwood Baptist Church, I quickly became aware of the fact that written history had not told me all there was to know. I was soon to discover that the church had some storms to blow and had been guilty of some terrible sins; but these incidents in history had either been left out, smoothed over, or swept under the rug. But the church of the Acts of the Apostles, before it could be empowered with the Holy Spirit, had to deal with its own failures and the failures of those who were once a part of them. No church today can expect to be power-centered unless it is able to come to grips with its failures and of those who have been a part of it.

Peter stood up among the 120 and preached a sermon about "Judas who was guide to those who arrested Jesus." Then he cited the real tragedy of Judas for he says, "For he was numbered among us, and was allotted his share in this ministry" (Acts 1:17). Judas was part of "the twelve" who had been charged to do service in the ministry of the Gospel of Jesus Christ. Peter said, "...he was numbered among us" i.e., (the word used here is $\kappa\alpha\tau\eta\rho\iota\theta\mu\eta\mu\acute{\epsilon}\nu o\varsigma$=*katerithmamenos*, a similar word for that which is used for arithmetic), he was added by Jesus via his arithmetical process to the number of disciples to make them twelve. In other words, Jesus saw some value and virtue in Judas enough to add him to his band of disciples. Judas betrayed not only the Lord for the thirty pieces of silver which he got, he betrayed the Lord's trust in himself. Judas was greedy for gold. He lusted for land. He was not worthy of Jesus' trust. This was not the kind of man the Lord could use in a power-centered church; so God let a terrible calamity come upon him. He purchased a parcel of land with the gold he had gotten from his ill-conceived betrayal of Jesus; but, the story is that after purchasing the land, he fell headlong and burst open in the middle, his bowels gushed out and he died. This was the tragedy of Judas. It just may be that today's church fails to be power-centered because there are too many Judases who are greedy for gold, lovers of land, and betrayers of trust. I do not know about any of the churches where you brethren pastor, but I pastored a church where there were people who were greedy for gold. They thought nothing of working on two or three jobs or doing a little bit of everything (even though their ethical and spiritual values were seriously in question) in order to make some money. And, it does not matter if such a job, or the many jobs they had, called for working on Sunday, even when it is not necessary to do so. They were simply greedy for gold, so they worked on Sunday to get it.

Then there are those who are lovers of land. They have worked to buy a nice house in the suburbs; so now that they have to keep their house clean and their lawn mowed and manicured, they don't have time for the worship of the Lord or the work of the church. These people cannot be a part of the power-centered church; for they are not there when they are needed, they are busy satisfying their greed for gold and lust for land. The work is too great, the road is too rough, and the going is too tough for a person who has money on his mind, houses in his head, and betrayal in his bosom. This was the kind of fellow Judas was, and the Lord allowed something terrible to happen to him just as he will allow something terrible to happen to any person whom he adds to his fellowship through his arithmetical process, but who turns aside because of his greed for gold, lust for land, and bent to betrayal.

Once the disciples had worked through the agony of their failure in Judas, they set before them two men, Joseph called Barsabbas, whose surname was Justus, and Matthias. They prayed again and asked the Lord:

> Thou, Lord, which knowest the hearts of all men, shew whether of these two thou hast chosen, That he may take part of this ministry and apostleship, from which Judas by transgression fell, that he might go to his own place. (Acts 1:24f)

Notice, they prayed and asked the Lord to show them the one whom He had chosen; they were not making the selection themselves, "...shew whether of these two thou hast chosen...." I think this method calls into question the way many of our churches call their pastors; some on the basis of how well the preacher can whoop; some on the basis of how well the preacher can pull the strings of politics; and, some on the basis of whether they can buy their own way into the office.[17] But these brethren of the church of the Acts of the Apostles, a church that was on its way to becoming power-centered, asked the Lord to "...shew whether of these two thou has chosen." When they had cast lots, the lot fell on Matthias, and he was enrolled with the eleven disciples.

So when the eleven disciples and the other 120 members in the Upper Room had taken care of their organizational business, when they had gotten everything together, then the Lord fulfilled his promise to send the Holy Spirit in power. When the day of Pentecost came, the disciples were together in the Upper Room. Suddenly, there came a sound from heaven like a mighty wind. It filled the whole house. There appeared to them tongues of fire that rested upon each of them; and, all were filled with the Holy Spirit and spoke in tongues as the Spirit gave them utterance.

Now there are at least four things of importance that

---

[17]The contemporary National Baptist congregation plays a critical role in the selection, what we refer to as the "call," of a pastor. We solicit candidates, evaluate their resume, hear them preach, and then vote on the one who is to become pastor. This is an embellishment of the method used by the Early Church of the Acts of the Apostles. However, with the dimension of "prayer," the contemporary National Baptist church should never really have any problems with the pastor. The congregation will have made its selection and exercised its full authority in calling the person wanted for the position. Hence, if there were a problem subsequent to the call, the congregations surely bears just as much blame as anyone. The man "they called" was their choice, not God's.

evolved out of the coming of the Holy Spirit in power upon the church: (1) the Holy Spirit made it clear that the message of Jesus Christ must be communicated to all nations; (2) the Holy Spirit confirmed the faithfulness of the Word of God and His promise; (3) the Holy Spirit provoked a bold witness against sin and wickedness; and (4) the Holy Spirit revealed the inevitable victory of the church. Let me deal with each of these individually.

While the church was caught up in the Spirit, speaking in tongues, Luke says that the sound of that which was going on in the church caught the attention of a great multitude of people who had gathered to observe what was happening. The Evangelist says that they were "confounded, because every man heard them speaking in his own language." The crowd remarked that those who were speaking were all Galileans, but they were heard in their own language. Then Luke names off all the nations that were present: Parthians Medes, Elamites, residents of Mesopotamia, Judea and Cappadocia, Pontus, and Asia, Phrygia and Pamphylia, Egypt and parts of Libya and Cyrene, Jews and proselytes from Rome, Cretans and Arabians, all heard what the disciples were saying in their own tongues of the mighty work of God.

This is the power-centered church, a church which bears a message of the mighty works of God which is heard and understood by the nations of the world. The power-centered church recognizes that the Gospel is not limited to the people of one's own clime and time; it recognizes that the Gospel is not provincial, parochial, and regionally regimented; the church that is centered in power is that church which takes seriously Jesus' Great Commission when he said, "go ye therefore, and teach all nations, baptizing them in the Name of the Father, and of the Son, and of the Holy Ghost; Teaching them to observe all things whatsoever I have commanded you." The power-centered church takes this seriously and goes into all the world preaching the Gospel, believing that people in a strange land will hear the Good News in their own tongue.

The second thing of significance which evolved out of the coming of the Holy Spirit in power upon to the church of the Acts of the Apostles was that it was confirmed in the mind of the disciples of the faithfulness of God's Word and promise. Jesus had told the disciples to go back to Jerusalem and wait for the coming of the promise of the Father. That promise would be the baptizing of the Holy Spirit which was promised in Joel 2:28-32. When, as Luke reports, some of the onlookers remarked that the disciples were filled with new wine, Peter stood in their midst and reminded them that it was only the third hour of the day. Then he told them that ". . .this is that which was spoken by the prophet Joel; it shall come to pass in the last days, saith God, that I will pour out my Spirit upon all flesh: and your sons and your daughters shall prophesy, and your young men shall see visions, and your old men shall dream dreams" (Acts 2:16ff). For Peter and the disciples, God's word of promise had been confirmed.

The power-centered church lives in anticipation of the fulfillment of God's promise; in other words, the power-centered church is a hoping church, a church which waits in hope on the fulfillment of God's promise. And when the promise comes, the power-centered church recognizes it without question.

The third thing of importance which evolved out of the coming of the Holy Spirit upon the church of the Acts of the Apostles was its prompting of the disciples to witness against sin and wickedness. When Peter had preached God's promise that had been foretold in the

Book of Joel of the Old Testament, he turned his message to address the crime that was done at Calvary. Peter said:

> Ye men of Israel, hear these words: Jesus of Nazareth, a man approved of God among you by miracles and wonders and signs, which God did by him in the midst of you, as ye yourselves know: Him being delivered by the determinate counsel and foreknowledge of God, ye have taken, and by wicked hands have crucified and slain. (Acts 2:22-23)

Now, this was something! Here, Peter was standing in the midst of Jews who could have been a part of the crucifixion of Jesus on Calvary, or certainly were related by their Jewish blood and religion to those who crucified Him, and yet he, without fear or trepidation, laid the charge before them that it was they who had crucified Jesus and killed him by the hands of lawless men. Peter was placing his life on the line by proclaiming such a message and making such strong charges; but, this he did. This is the character of the power-centered church; it is willing to take the risk of telling it like it is; of speaking the truth in spite of the consequences; of addressing crime, wickedness and sin no matter who it may affect or what might be the result. With the fiery tongues of the Holy Spirit yet burning in his bosom, Peter went out and unrelentingly told the Jews that they were guilty of committing the crime and abominable sin of crucifying Jesus at Calvary on that dark Friday.

At this point the church of the Acts of the Apostles sits in serious judgment on the contemporary church. The contemporary church lacks the power not only to witness to sinners about the saving grace of the Lord Jesus, it lacks the power to witness against the sin, wickedness, and crime in our day. I remember very clearly when the Vietnam War began, there were cries of moral outrage from many quarters of the nation and the world. Students on college campuses were enraged that our nation would enter into a war on the other side of the globe, a war that would certainly claim some of their lives, without any clear-cut reason. None of our shores were threatened. Democracy was not challenged; and yet, America entered into a war where she could gain nothing, but lose everything. There were cries in some sectors of the nation about America's ulterior motives, *viz.*, her greed for the oil which lay off the shores of Vietnam and her desire to monopolize the rice business in Vietnam (eg., Samuel Yette's *The Choice*). There were cries from many quarters in opposition to that evil and immoral war; but, there was no cry from the church. Billy Graham openly supported the war. Many churches and national religious bodies held stock in businesses and industries associated with the Military Industrial Complex, which supplied the war with material such as napalm, bombs, and bullets. In the face of this international crime, the church was silent. It had no power to speak. When Martin Luther King, Jr. spoke against the Vietnam War from the pulpit of Riverside Church in New York City, calling America the greatest purveyor of evil in the world, the church tried to quiet him and insisted he was talking too much. Even his closest friends said he had gone too far by denouncing America for her part in the war. Of course, when that happened, when the church showed that it did not have the power to speak against evil, even when it is done by its own country, when it was clear that Martin Luther King, Jr. did not have the support of his fellow churchmen, the world killed him. This was a time when the church showed itself not to have power, but smitten with weakness indeed.

I do not think the Black church can escape this

condemnation. Some atrocious things are happening to our people in South Africa. Our Black brothers and sisters are enslaved in their own homeland; they are experiencing the kind of slavery we knew in this country a little over a hundred years ago. And yet, although we know what it means to be enslaved, the Black church has not raised a hue and cry against such flagrant treatment of Black human beings in South Africa. I do not hear this theme addressed in our national conventional gatherings or in our prestigious publications. Maybe here and there a voice cries out; but the Black church as a whole is not raising her voice against the crimes of Apartheid in South Africa. This is a clear sign of a church where power has taken leave of its center. When Peter preached his sermon on the day of Pentecost, he raised his voice against the crime of the Jews at Calvary. He said, "You crucified [Jesus] and killed [Him] by the hands of lawless men" (Acts 2:23b RSV, emphasis mine). Peter had the courage and power to say this because he was a part of a church that had power, power endowed by the Holy Spirit.

Finally, the last thing of significance that evolved out of the coming of the Holy Spirit on the Day of Pentecost was the revelation of the inevitable victory of the church. The truth of this is cast in the light of the death and resurrection of Jesus as it was preached in Peter's sermon on the Day of Pentecost. Peter found new hope and promise for the inevitable victory of the church and for remaking the world for the good of humanity through the resurrection of Jesus. In his tremendous sermon that day, Peter referred to Jesus, His mighty works and wonders and signs which God did through Him, and the fact that He was delivered up according to the plan and foreknowledge of God, and was crucified and killed by the hands of lawless men. But then, Peter says something startling and marvelous altogether: He says, "Whom God hath raised up, having loosed the pains of death: because it was not possible that he should be holden of it" (Acts 2:24). The Holy Spirit had now shown Peter that there was something about the certainty, the inevitability of the resurrection, so much so that he said, ". . .it was not possible for [Jesus] to be held by [death and the grave]" (RSV). Peter harks back to the Messianic Psalm, Psalm 16:8-11, where it says, "Because thou wilt not leave my soul in hell, neither wilt thou suffer thine Holy One to see corruption." Peter now sees, through the revelation of the Holy Spirit and the power that came on the Day of Pentecost, that there was nothing that could have kept Jesus in the grave, for it did not have the power to hold him. There was another and greater power over death and the grave. That power was God.

I really do not think we get the force of what Peter is saying here until we take another look at how well the enemy planned the crucifixion of Jesus and how, in spite of all that was done, he still was raised from the grave. Before the enemy crucified Jesus, they first tried to discredit him. During his trial before Pilate, they dressed him in a purple robe and placed upon his head a crown of thorns in mockery and derision, to set him out as a fake and a phoney, a king which had no regality or authority. Out at Calvary, they wrote in derision above the cross, "Jesus of Nazareth, the King of the Jews." I like the way Chunky Harvey of Greenwood Baptist Church in Tuskegee, Alabama once put it when he said, that they tried to humiliate Jesus by nailing his hands and riveting his feet and lifting him up between the heavens and the earth and placing him between two thieves as if to box him in and say, "We got you now and you won't get away." Then they took him down and placed him in a tomb that had been hewn out of a rock (one Black preacher said they put the Rock within a rock). The Pharisees went in to Pilate on the day after the Day of Preparation and said to him, "Sir, we remember how that impostor said, while he was still alive, 'After three days I will rise again.' Therefore, order the sepulchre to be made secure until the third day, lest his disciples go and steal him away, and tell the people, 'He has risen from the dead,' and the last fraud will be worse that the first" (Matthew 27:63ff., RSV). Then Pilate said to the Pharisees, "You have a guard of soldiers; go, make it as secure as you can [or, make it as secure as you know how]" (RSV).

The Pharisees sent Roman soldiers to the tomb, and they made the sepulchre secure; they sealed the tomb with a Roman seal which was to be broken by no one, and, they stood guard over the tomb. They thought they had Jesus in the grave. All night Friday, he laid there. All day Saturday, Jesus, stayed in the tomb. All night Saturday, he stayed in the tomb. Peter says in his Epistle that Jesus did take leave in the Spirit to go down into the regions of Hell to preach the Gospel to the spirits there. But Saturday night, Jesus was in the tomb. The devil still thought he had Jesus. But early Sunday morning, the First Day of the Week, something began to happen in that graveyard. Matthew's Gospel says that while Mary Magdalene and the other Mary were on their way to the grave, an earthquake shook the grave; and behold, an angel of the Lord descended from heaven and came and rolled back the stone, and sat upon it. The Roman guards who stood watch over the grave trembled with fear and became as dead men. The angel said to the women, "Fear not ye: for I know that ye seek Jesus, which was crucified. He is not here: for he has risen, as he said" (Mt. 28:5f RSV) according to the plan of God. Paul came along later and recognized that God had raised Jesus in "power and glory."

The point here is that the enemies of Jesus did all the dirty and lowdown things they could to humiliate and disgrace Jesus before they killed him. And after they killed him at Calvary, they did all they could to keep him in the grave. But, all they could do was not enough, for early on Sunday morning, God raised up Jesus from the grave in power and glory.

So in Peter's sermon on the Day of Pentecost, he showed the new theological meaning of the resurrection of Jesus, i.e., that "God hath raised him up, having loosed the pains of death: because it was not possible [it was not in God's plan] that he should be holden of it." And now, since Jesus had given the church the mandate to witness in His name, and since the church had been empowered by the Holy Spirit, Peter was beginning to see that not only was the grave unable to hold Jesus, but the powers of death would not be able to hold the church. The historical "impossible possibility" of the resurrection of Jesus was now to become the "impossible possibility" of the church. Nothing would be able to stop the church. Nothing would be able to stop the church because it was in God's plan for it to be victorious. Jesus said in Matthew 16:18, ". . .on this rock I will build my church, and the powers of death shall not prevail against it."

In the Acts of the Apostles, Luke shows at least three ways the church moved along its trajectory as an unstoppable movement for righteousness, on its way to an inevitable victory. The first is in his citation of the tremendous membership increase of the church in spite of the terrific opposition. Over and over, Luke refers to the growth of the church. In Acts 2:41, he says, after Peter had finished his powerful sermon on the Day of

Pentecost that, "...and there were added unto them about three thousand souls." And he closes out that chapter by saying, "And the Lord added to the church daily such as should be saved" (Acts 2:47). In chapter four, verses 1-4, Luke cites the fact that the Priests, and captain of the temple and the Sadducees came upon Peter and John, after they had healed the lame man at the Beautiful Gate of the temple; and they arrested the two disciples and kept them in jail for the night. But the record reads that in spite of this oppression by the Jews, "...the number of the men was about five thousand." Then after the apostles had appointed seven men to take charge of the work of serving tables in chapter six, when they had held the ceremony of prayer and laying hands upon the seven, Luke says, "And the word of God increased; and the number of the disciples multiplied in Jerusalem greatly, and a great company of the priests were obedient to the faith" (Acts 6:7). The church was increasing even by taking into her membership those priests of the temple who had persecuted her just a short time before. God gave the church tremendous ability to win over and add those people of the world who had previously been her persecutors.

No clearer example is seen than that of Saul who came to be known as Paul. In Acts 8:1, we are introduced to Saul when Luke says that "Saul, was consenting unto [Stephen's] death." Then the entire ninth chapter is given to Paul's conversion. Acts 9:1-2 says, "And Saul, yet breathing out threatnings and slaughter against the disciples of the Lord, went unto the high priests, And desired him letters to Damascus to the synagogues, that if he found any of this Way, whether they were men or women, he might bring them bound unto Jerusalem." Then the dramatic story of Paul's conversion on the Damascus Road ensues; and Luke closes out the story by saying, "Then had the churches rest throughout all Judea and Galilee and Samaria, and were edified; and walking in the fear of the Lord, and in the comfort of the Holy Ghost, were multiplied" (Acts 9:31). Then as Paul and Silas passed through Asia Minor on their second missionary journey in Acts 16:5, it is said that "And so were the churches established in the faith, and increased in number daily." On and on and on, Luke goes citing the tremendous increase in the number of converts who were added to the church. This is his way of pointing up the inevitable victory of the church, by citing how the church grew in numbers.

I think it is important to point out that Luke's citation of the numbers of people who were added to the church was not his way of being flippant or boastful; but, it was his way of showing how the church was to demonstrate the power God had added to the movement in spite of the adversity through which it was going. It seemed that the more adversity the church experienced, the more God added to the movement. The more the church was punished for witnessing to the Name of Jesus the Christ, the more the power of God was manifested to believers, adding them to the ranks of the righteous. But I am afraid that the church today has altered the plan of God and has made use of other means by which people enter. People join the church today rather than being added by God. And, they join a church on the basis of some slick advertisement campaign. It is not the adversity that the church has endured, but advertisements that lure people into the church. And they join the church; they are not added, they join. But in many cases of which I know, as soon as the novelty and emotional excitement wear off, or as soon as hard times press in upon a church, those persons who joined soon un-join themselves and go and join another where there is better advertisement and more excitement; and, some people have been known to simply go from church to church, "joining" the church. But according to the Acts of the Apostles, members were not added to the church through advertisement, they were added through and in spite of adversity. Adversity was one of the reasons for the growth of the church.

One other way Luke shows how unstoppable was the church, its inevitable victory and the fact that the powers of death would not be able to hold it, was in his stories of the miraculous release of the apostles from imprisonment for preaching the Word of God. In the twelfth chapter of Acts, it is said that Herod the king laid violent hands upon some within the church. The report is that he killed James, the brother of John, with the edge of the sword. When he saw that it pleased the Jews, he proceeded to arrest Peter also. Look what he did to Peter. He placed him in prison and put him under a guard of four squads of soldiers. Luke goes on to say—it seems in passing but certainly to make the point—that earnest prayer was made for him (Peter) to God by the church. Luke goes on to describe the scene in the prison. He says that Peter was asleep between two soldiers, bound with two chains, and sentries were at the door guarding the prison. But then an angel of the Lord appeared to Peter in prison, a light shone in the cell and the seraph visitor smote Peter on the side and woke him from his sleep. Immediately, his chains fell off and he was told to dress himself. Notice that in all of this, the soldiers were still asleep. Peter did as he was told and followed the angel. Luke dramatically describes that Peter and the angel passed through the first and the second guard. They came to an iron gate which led into the city of Jerusalem. When they got to the gate, the Bible says, "It opened to them of its own accord" (Acts 12:10). It sounds like magic, but it was not magic; it was the movement of the power of God. This was God's way of showing Peter and the church that nothing would stand in their way. Gates that stood before the church locked securely, would open of their own accord.

Finally, Luke shows the inevitable victory of the church by reporting that after Paul had reached Rome to be tried before the great tribunal of Roman justice, that even in Rome, the church could not be stopped. Luke says, as he closes out the Book of Acts that, "[Paul] dwelt two whole years in his own hired house, and received all who came in unto him, Preaching the kingdom of God, and teaching those things which concern the Lord Jesus Christ, with all confidence, no man forbidding him" (Acts 28:30-31 KJV).

And this was what it came to mean by the resurrection of Jesus when Peter said that it was not possible for the grave to hold Him. It meant that nothing could hold the church, for it was in the plan of God for it to rise above wretchedness, walk over wickedness, and march through military might. Nothing could stop the church, because it possessed a center of power.

I think of the movement of the church as likened to the movement of the Mississippi River. The Mississippi River begins its powerfully majestic course as it flows out of the northern end of Lake Itasco in North Central Minnesota. The mighty Mississippi River begins as a trickling stream only ten feet wide and less than two feet deep (you can walk across the Mississippi River at its point of origin). But as the Mississippi River makes its way southward, it passes the twin cities of Minneapolis and St. Paul in Minnesota; it flows on through Wisconsin, and passes on by Dubuque and Davenport in Iowa. Its laughing waves elude the grasping clutches of old St. Louis in Missouri; it rushes on by the grand old bluff city of Memphis in Tennessee, and by the time she meanders into the idyllic State of Mississippi, the old Negro sat on its banks and looked admiringly at it and said, "That old man River, just keeps rolling along." That old river keeps rolling until she gets down to Baton Rouge in Louisiana; and then on to New Orleans where she begins to find her long-sought-for freedom in the open spaces and the leaping waves of the Gulf of Mexico. Nothing can stand in the way of the mighty Mississippi River.

Like that old man River, the mighty Mississippi, the church has kept rolling along. Nothing has been able to hold it and keep it from making its way through history. It made its impact on the Holy City of Jerusalem; it left its mark on Judea, and changed the lifestyle in Samaria. It went into Asia Minor, breaking down barriers, hurtling over walls of opposition. It came to Rome, saw the Imperial City and brought it to her knees. It conquered the nations of Europe and enthralled the isles of Great Britain; and today, Christianity is spreading and Christians are being won all over the world. Nothing stood in the path of the movement of the church because it was endowed with power from on high. And the glory of the church is that one day it too, like that mighty Mississippi River, will reach its final destiny when it finds rest in the bosom of God. I believe it is the church of which John was speaking when he says:

> "...I saw the holy city, new Jerusalem, coming down out of heaven from God, prepared as a bride adorned for her husband; and I heard a loud voice from the throne saying, 'Behold, the dwelling of God is with men. He will dwell with them, and they shall be his people, and God himself will be with them; he will wipe away every tear from their eyes, and death shall be no more, neither shall there be mourning nor crying nor pain any more, for the former things have passed away.'" (Rev. 21:2-4)

It is this kind of church, a church with a center of power and an unfolding drama destined for the victor's circle, of which we are a part.

Chapter IV

THE CHURCH OF POWER: A MONOLITH OF MULTIPLES

The church of the Acts of the Apostles was truly a church of power. She was such because of the fruit she bore and the manner by which she bore that fruit. The incredible story of the Acts of the Apostles is that in spite of all the attempts to crush the movement, the church marched invincibly forward conquering everything in her path, capturing the imagination of the people, and adding thousands of disparate personalities to her fold.

The church of the Acts of the Apostles became a movement of power because God gave her the wisdom and wherewithal to forge herself into a monolith of multiples. It is instructive to note that at the outset of Luke's history of the Early Church, mention is made of the names of the eleven disciples of Jesus (*see*, Acts 1:13). The eleven had returned to Jerusalem and the Upper Room. Those who gathered were Peter and John, James and Andrew, Philip and Thomas, Bartholomew and Matthew, James the son of Alphaeus, and Simon the Zealot, and Judas the son of James. Notice the disparate personality of them all. Peter was the impetuous one, a rough-hewn fisherman with cursings and obscenities on his tongue, and prone to violence. Thomas was the doubter, who demanded evidence that Jesus was the resurrected Christ. Matthew was the tax collector who was despised by his fellow Jews, for Tiberius Caesar had imposed taxes on the Holy Land for the benefit of the Roman Empire. Simon was the Zealot, known for notorious violence and sabre-rattling behavior. The rest fell in between. Another was to be added to this number, and somehow the Holy Spirit was able to perform an amalgamation of these disparate personalities so that when they gathered in the Upper Room they all were together in mind and body. It is important to remember that these were the leaders of the church whom Jesus was sending out into a tremendously unsettled and turbulent world. But before they could be sent out, they had to overcome their disparate ways and be forged into a monolith of multiples, they would have different names and different backgrounds, but they would be forged together as a mighty monolith in spite of their disparate ways. Therefore, as the Lord had directed, they gathered in the Upper Room where the Holy Spirit performed the amalgamation process.

This is the first key to how the present-day church can become the power the Lord designed her to be; the leaders of the church must be forged into a mighty monolith, providing the cutting edge for those who follow. If this is done, the inevitable results will follow; the church will be an invincible power in the world, capturing and conquering everything in her path. If this is not done at the outset, or corrective action taken at some point along her trajectory, then all she does will be nothing more than sounding brass and a tinkling cymbal. The calamity of division will be her lot.

Because the Twelve gave themselves to prayer as they had been directed by the Lord, they were empowered by the Holy Spirit so much so that they were able to overcome their personal differences. Luke captures the theological significance of this "togetherness" by using the word ὁμοῦ=*homou* (Acts 2:1) or its variable ὁμοθυμαδὸν= *homothumadon*. Through the empowerment of the Holy Spirit, the Early Church of the Acts of the Apostles developed a spirit of togetherness, of oneness of mind. In chapter one, verse fourteen, Luke says that "All these with one accord [ὁμοθυμαδὸν =*homothumadon*; can also be translated "with one mind" or "as one man"] devoted themselves to prayer." Luke continues to pick up this phenomenon when he discloses that in chapter two, verse one, "When the day of Pentecost had come, they were all *together* [ὁμου=*homou*] in one place" (emphasis mine). In chapter two, after Simon Peter had preached his powerful sermon, Luke says that the ones who became believers along with the Twelve had all things in common; they sold their possessions and goods and distributed them to everyone as each had need. Then Luke says that they were in the temple daily together (ὁμοθυμαδὸν = *homothumadon*, "with one mind," Acts 2:46). Again in chapter four, verse twenty-four, the theme of togetherness of mind is cited by Luke. Peter and John had been arrested for healing the lame man at the Gate called Beautiful. When they had been released, they returned to the members of the church. Luke says they "lifted up their voices *together*" (emphasis mine). In chapter five, following the tragic incident of Ananias and Sapphira, Luke again says the church was "all together"(ὁμοθυμαδὸν = *homothumadon*, "with one mind") in Solomon's portico. Finally, Luke states that when the church had been scattered about, Philip went down to the city of Samaria and proclaimed Christ to them. As he preached Christ in Samaria, Luke says that "the multitudes with one accord [ὁμοθυμαδὸν = *homothumadon*, "with one mind"] gave heed to what was said by Philip" (Acts 8:6).

So then, what we have reconstructed from Luke's theology is a church in the Acts of the Apostles which is characterized by togetherness and oneness of mind. This was truly a church of power. Through its willingness to give itself to prayer, the power of the Holy Spirit came upon them so that they were given oneness of mind that the church might express its witness in the same words and the same way. Incredible! Yes, it is incredible to think that the Holy Spirit wielded so much power that He could cause the differing opinions and mind-sets of the twelve disciples to become one. And just as incredible, they all were saying the same thing.

It could be that the reason the church of today is so bereft of power is that in its multiplicity of expressions, she is not able to get herself together to think the same thing and say the same thing. All of the many denominations which dot the hillsides across the land are like trumpets that give forth an uncertain and different sound. Each has its own theology, ecclesiology, and soteriology. Many denominations are forever arguing over the correct day on which Christians should worship. Others are obsessed with the notion that church structure must conform to their own or it is not structured correctly. Then there are others who insist that salvation is dependent on one's identification with that particular church or denomination. And so, listening to the loud and disparate dinning which comes from the various communities which *call* themselves the church, one becomes strangely confused because of dissimilar signals. The result of it all is that church memberships are shrinking and the once rippling flow of new converts into the church is now drying up. It is no secret that today every major denomination is recording a radical decline in attendance in Sunday schools.

It all is happening because Christian couriers of the Gospel cannot get themselves together and simultaneously speak the same thing. In the Acts of the Apostles, Luke unfolds for us the thrilling drama of an unstoppable church which lurched over barriers and leaped over obstacles and moved as a mighty monolith of multiples because she got herself together and was empowered by the Holy Spirit to have the same mind and speak the same thing.

It is no small thing to note that in the Early Church strong emphasis was placed on the need for oneness of men and mind. The Apostle Paul, the first of New Testament writers, emphasized the sameness of mind in virtually all his correspondence with the nascent churches born through his ministry. To the Philippians, he passionately pleaded for them to "Fulfill ye my joy, that ye be likeminded, having the same love, being of one accord, of one mind" (Phil. 2:2 KJV). So vehemently did he think the church must speak the same thing and be of the same mind that he pronounced anathema, a curse, on anyone who dared to speak anything different from what he had taught. Particularly is this painfully stated in the Galatian letter where Paul said:

> I marvel that ye are so soon removed from him that called you into the grace of Christ unto another gospel: Which is not another; but there be some that trouble you, and would pervert the gospel of Christ. But though we, or an angel from heaven, preach any other gospel unto you than that which we have preached unto you, let him be accursed. (Gal. 1:6ff KJV)

In Our Lord's High Priestly Prayer in John 17:11, Jesus prays, "Holy Father, keep through thine own name, those whom thou hast given me, that they may be one, as we are."

In both cases, with Paul and Jesus in His prayer, the appeal is that the members of the church be one in body and mind. The churches to which Paul preached were faced with a history bitterly flavored with suffering and persecution. The Neronian Persecution came upon the church in the late 50's and early A.D. 60's. There was no way she could withstand the ferocity of Nero's wrath and survive to tell about it were togetherness and singleness of mind not foremost in her character. The Gospel of John was written about A.D. 95., and so were the words of Jesus' prayer set down in that time. It was the time of emperor Domitian's persecution of the church; it was the time when John of the Revelation suffered exile on the isle of Patmos for preaching the Word of the Lord. This being the case, it becomes clear the meaning of Jesus' prayer. He prayed for oneness on the part of the disciples. He knew that the church of which they were a part could never withstand the mania of Domitian, which issued forth in battles with wild beasts and appointments with death on a flaming pile while bound to a stake. Oneness of body and mind within the church, for Jesus and Paul, would be enough to ferry it through the flame and flood of persecution in any time or clime.

The history of the Christian church is spattered about with burgeoning moments when she failed to live up to her calling to be a Spirit-empowered monolith of multiples, speaking with one mind. There is no better example of this and the time when the church manifested herself in tragic anemia rather than standing the test and triumphing in power than that of the time of Hitler's Nazi Regime. The church in Germany during the time of Hitler almost totally abdicated her role. She fastened herself to the notorious Hitler for the sake of her own survival rather than raise a unified prophetic voice against his murderous scheme of Jewish genocide. There is at least one other moment in the history of the Christian church when there came forth from the camp a strange and uneven sound. It was the Martin Luther King, Jr. Era when, through the Gospel of Jesus Christ and the church, he tried to secure the civil rights of Black people in America. Martin Luther King, Jr.'s letter from the Birmingham jail clearly discloses that although he had lifted from the pages of the Bible the motifs of freedom and attempted to allow the Word to become flesh, there were differing opinions within the religious community of Birmingham, Alabama, both Jewish and Gentile, of what the Gospel meant when it came to freedom for oppressed Blacks in America. Because the church did not have the peculiar oneness of body and mind that so strongly characterized the Early Church of the Acts of the Apostles, it was nothing for the enemy of righteousness to slay the dreamer. The purveyors of evil in the larger American community was that such engagements would never elicit a unified outcry from the community called the church. And so the church, divided and anemic, hid herself while she whimpered and whispered her lament.

When the times are out of joint and society is turned bottomside up as it was in Germany during the Hitler Era and the Civil Rights Era of Martin Luther King, Jr., it is lamentable that the church chose to assume a posture of weakness as a witness and to travel the road of life clothed in the pious raiment of anemia. Such was not the case with the church of the Acts of the Apostles. Faced with a world wreaking with miasmic misery, jaded with injustice, reeling from rottenness, dogged by demons and the Devil, pressured by Roman politics, and confused by the chaos of ten thousand different religions converging upon her at the same time, the church of the Acts of the

Apostles rose to the occasion, empowered by the Spirit of God obtained through the medium of prayer and met headlong her opposition as a monolith of multiples. And though being many, it had that essential oneness of body and mind.

There is another dimension within the Acts of the Apostles which clearly sets the church as a power because of its composition as a monolith of multiples. That dimension was the ability to be a church for all peoples, a church that truly knew what it meant to be an integration of the nations of the world and a combination of the cultures of society. Luke powerfully captures the mind of the reader with this fact when early in his story of the Early Church, in the second chapter of the Acts of the Apostles, he lists the names of all the nations who were caught up in the rapture of the Holy Spirit on the Day of Pentecost. Luke records that on the Day of Pentecost, "...there were dwelling at Jerusalem Jews, devout men, out of every nation under heaven" (Acts 2:5 KJV). But this is not enough, he painstakingly names them all: **Parthians and Medes and Elamites and residents of Mesopotamia, Judea and Cappadocia, Pontus and Asia, Phrygia and Pamphylia, Egypt and the Parts of Libya belonging to Cyrene, and visitors from Rome, Cretans and Arabians** (*see*, Acts 2:9-11).

These all had gathered in Jerusalem and were enthralled with a strangely enchanting air of expectancy. Something excitingly strange and enchanting did happen, for while the disciples in the Upper Room were being showered with the power of the Holy Spirit and were ecstatically speaking in the tongues of glossolalia, the people of the gathered nations heard each of them in their own tongue. Luke expressed the phenomenon like this:

> Now when this was noised abroad, the multitude came together, and were confounded, because that every man heard them speak in his own language. And they were amazed and marvelled, saying one to another, 'Behold, are not all these which speak Galileans? And how hear we every man in our own tongue, wherein we were born?' (Acts 2:6-8 KJV)

Amazing! Incredible! But, altogether true! What was impossible with man became the impossible possibility with God. In a world where the variation of languages of man was as commonplace as the cacophony of sound which bursts forth from birds of the forest, God caused the Spirit-filled utterance of the disciples at Pentecost to be understood by all the nations of the world. What a marvel!

The church of the Acts of the Apostles never seems to cease in its challenge of the contemporary church. All too often, the contemporary church finds herself unable to speak and be understood as a people empowered by God's Spirit, not only by the nations of the world, but by those within the church herself. Such was the case with the grandmother of the venerable sage and mystic, Howard Thurman. Thurman's grandmother, who was a slave in the state of Florida, never understood the mouthings of the White plantation preacher as he passionately urged the slaves to be obedient to their masters. It was a strange and uneven sound, one which Thurman's grandmother never wanted to hear. Her experience with that uncertain sound coming from the White church caused her to reject forever, everything written by the Apostle Paul, with the exception of his hymn of love in the thirteenth chapter of 1 Corinthians. Such a strange and uncertain sound was heard by Frederick Douglass when on Sunday morning he saw his overseer going to church with his Bible under his arm, only to be confronted with that same man on Monday morning with cursings and obscenities leaping from his mouth. The Jews of Nazi Germany heard the unintelligible sound when demonically devout Christians shouted murderous blasphemies as they marched the children of David to their death in seething gas chambers and blistering ovens.

The fiercely religious Iranians of our day are aghast with mental confusion from the sounds of jangled discord that freely issue forth from a "Christian" America, a nation that is mired in an intransigent and stubborn unwillingness to confess to the mountains of atrocities which have been heaped upon the head of its international Iranian neighbor. Yes, the church of the Acts of the Apostles stands in critical judgment of her contemporary American counterpart for her unwillingness to be empowered by the Holy Spirit, so that it can speak as the church and be understood by its national neighbors as it was on the Day of Pentecost. It is a criticism well worth pondering and a challenge well worth accepting by the present-day church; for without the ability to speak and be understood by the nations of the world, her missionary edge is severely dulled, rendering it unable and incapable of cutting through the wilderness of this world.

But Luke does not desist with this one account of the church's ability to mold into a monolith for God the nations of the world. Like the rhythmic waves of the marching sea that crash upon the shore in calculated cadence, Luke tells of how God added to the church the peoples of the nations of the world. By the time we get to the sixth chapter of Acts, we are told that there were Hellenists (Jews of Greek culture) as well as Hebrews numbered among the members of the church. Following Luke's announcement of the diaspora, the dispersion of the disciples of the church throughout the Roman Empire and the world, he tells us in chapter eight that Philip went down to a city in Samaria. Samaria of all places; it was the homeland of those sons of Israel who had been rejected and disowned by the Jews. But Philip, himself a Hellenistic Jew now become Christian, went down to Samaria with audacity that only the Holy Spirit could give. It is proclaimed by Luke that Philip preached Christ to them, and there was much joy in that city.

Defying all the cultural and social, credal and legal mandates of racial discrimination, the Holy Spirit arranged it so that Ethiopia would "stretch out her hands to God" (Psalm 68:31). The promptings of the Holy Spirit led Philip to a desolate road to Gaza where he came upon an Ethiopian eunuch, a nobleman of the court of Candace, the queen of Ethiopia. A sermon that announced Jesus the Christ as the fulfillment of Old Testament scripture would be enough to convert this Black man from Ethiopia and add him to the church.

The story of God's miraculous drama of forming a church of multiples moves on. In chapter ten, Simon Peter's prejudice against Gentiles is swept away like dust. While reposing on a housetop in Joppa, Simon Peter saw in a dream a host of animals that for any Jew was consigned to uncleanness. Persistent in his piety, when Simon had been divinely ordered to rise and eat, he said, "Not so, Lord; for I have never eaten anything that is common or unclean" (Acts 10:14 KJV). The opportunity presented itself for God to declare to Simon that "What God hath cleansed, that call not thou common" (Acts 10:15 KJV). The stage was set for Simon Peter to meet Cornelius, a Gentile, a group the apostle formerly despised. Peter discovered that upon preaching the Gospel to Cornelius, this centurion as well was caught up in the Holy Spirit and became a candidate for baptism. Peter was driven to say

"Of a truth I perceive that God is no respecter of persons, But in every nation he that feareth him, and worketh righteousness, is accepted with him" (Acts 10:34).

But the Early Church was not simply made up of Gentiles and people of color who worshiped as pew members; these were also numbered among those who made up the theological and ecclesiological inner circle of the church. The point is clearly made when Luke takes us to the church of Antioch, where the followers of The Way were first called "Christians." Luke begins chapter thirteen by saying, "Now there were in the church that was at Antioch certain prophets and teachers; Barnabas, and Simeon who was called Niger, Lucius of Cyrene, and Manaen, which had been brought up with Herod the tetrarch, and Saul" (Acts 13:1). These were exhorted by the Holy Spirit to "Separate me Barnabas and Saul for the work whereunto I have called them" (Acts 13:2). After fasting and praying, these who were named laid hands upon Paul and Barnabas and sent them off on their first missionary journey.

It would be sufficient to state that at least two of the ecclesiastical staff of the church at Antioch were Black Africans; but a brief look at their native homeland would make the point more strongly. It can be assumed that Simeon called Niger was from the land called Niger. Niger was and still is today a country in the Northwest of the continent of Africa. It is, of course, inhabited by Black people. Luke states more specifically that Lucius was of Cyrene, that is to say, he was a native of the city of Cyrene. This city was located on the northern coast of Africa, in what is now the nation of Libya. Although the city was founded by the Greeks in the seventh century B.C., and came under Roman control later in history, and although Jews were carried there by Ptolemy I, sometime during the second century B.C., it is reasonable to conclude that the inhabitants were Black—as the Libyans of today—or certainly of a dark hue.

The point of this is that the church at Antioch was integrated in a very real sense, in the sense of color, race, and ethnic background. In the church at Antioch, the matter of color, race, and ethnic background made no difference, even when it came to administrative affairs. Through the authority vested in them by the Holy Spirit, these men of color took part in the laying on of hands on Paul and Barnabas in order to send them out into the world to be witnesses for the Lord. The sweep of the discussion here is that the Early Church possessed the unique distinction of having the ability to bring about an integration of the nations of the world and a combination of the cultures of society; it truly was a church for all people. In the Acts of the Apostles, there seems not to be even the slightest vestige of evidence that the difference in color, race, or ethnic background of men made any difference; they were all one in the sight of God. The fact that Luke cites the origin, the native land, of those of the ecclesiastical hierarchy of the church at Antioch, gives us a strong indication that their uniqueness and racial, ethnic, and cultural difference was acknowledged. But the fact that Luke cites them as a part of the inner circle, a part of those who made crucial decisions about the Kingdom's work, tells us that what differences they might have brought into the church as it regards color, race, and ethnic background, made no difference. These were a part of those whom Simon Peter discovered were also a part of God's moving drama of salvation; for he said, "Of a truth I perceive that God is no respecter of persons" (Acts 10:34f).

When this dimension of the Early Church is set before the church in America as it has been known unto this day, that which is representative of the Christian Faith is weighed in the balance and found wanting. While the Early Church of the Acts of the Apostles was founded as a monolith of multiples with a variety of vernacular, a combination of cultures and an array of races that manifested themselves in dynamic power, the church in America as it has been known unto this day has been warped and weakened because it has been ruptured by racism and its power eclipsed by cleavages of culture. It was by Divine design that all nations of the world, even the nations of the darker people of the world, would be a part of the Early Church as it began its dramatic movement through the world. No individual, regardless of race, color, culture, or ethnic background was despised, rejected, or relegated to an inferior status. All were important in the sight of God; in fact, all who received Jesus as the Christ, God gave them power to become sons of God. Jesus' plan for the composition of the Early Church was of such that not only would Black people of Ethiopia and Africa make up the membership of the congregation, they would be involved in the administrative and ecclesiastical decisions of the church as was the case in the church at Antioch. But this has been far from the case in the church as it has been known in America.

Had the church in America started as her forerunner in the Acts of the Apostles, she very well could be that spiritual entity of power that is so badly needed in a world that has been turned upside down. But this is not the case. The church in America began with a noble objective emblazoned on her soul, but she had one woeful weakness and a single fatal flaw. She considered Black people, the sons and daughters of Africa, unequal to White people. They concluded that Blacks were unfit to be children of God and members of the church. When it seemed feasible to evangelize Blacks as Christians, it was done clearly to make the sons and daughters of Africa more docile and effective slaves. There never was any sense of equality between Black Africans and White people in the early American church. Blacks were chattel, property, beasts, for certain less than human. At best they were slaves, forever to be consigned to be hewers of wood and drawers of water. This was how the church in America had its beginning.

As the movement of mythical freedom spread from sea to shining sea, the church did not get better in her relations with Black people. She got worse. This is evidenced by the fact that in 1845 or thereabout, years before the beginning of the Civil War between the North and the South over the issue of slavery, virtually every White denomination in America split over the same issue. Following the Civil War, there still was no amelioration of the condescending and paternalistic attitude of the White church toward Black people in America. Rejected and dehumanized on practically every hand, Black people sought to establish their own churches, associations, and conventions. When the American Publication Society refused to allow Black theologians to write articles and prepare lessons for their Sunday school literature, Black Baptists established their own publishing house so they could provide Sunday school literature for their own people. This situation has not changed dramatically to this day. While so-called integration of the races has taken place in America, the church today still is radically divided along the color lines of Black and White. In some instances, Blacks have been accepted, even sought, in White churches and denominations; but even in such cases, Blacks have not been allowed to write Sunday school lessons, prepare theologies, and develop programs for the church or denominations as a whole. Hardly has it been the case in White churches and denominations that Blacks have been permitted to enter the inner circle of administrative and ecclesiastical decision-making as was the case in the church at Antioch. About the only place in America where Black Christians have a semblance of authority in the church is within their own congregations and conventions.

Because the church in America has failed to follow its Lord, the resurrected Christ of the Acts of the Apostles and her first century archetype, to establish herself as a monolith of multiples, where everyone regardless of race, color, or ethnic background is equal and a brother, she has relegated herself to a posture of pitiful weakness. With the nation wrenched in the imbroglio of staggering crises—Iran, energy shortages, inflation and recession, rising racial temperatures and tensions, a society that simply has gone awry—it seems that the church would rise to the occasion as was the case with the Early Church of the Acts of the Apostles. But the church cannot! No one is seeking out the church for answers to any of the questions which today have rocked our nation on her heels. No one is listening to the feeble words the church attempts to pronounce. No one really cares, for there is aloft a troublesome feeling that because of its weakness there is no real difference the Christian church in America can make. The sadness is that at this point in time, such a conclusion smacks with so much truth. And it is so because the church of today, in all of her variety of expressions in America, has abandoned the plan laid out for her in the Acts of the Apostles to be a monolith of multiples.

While on a rare and coveted visit to India, Howard Thurman had the privilege of meeting the saintly Mahatma Gandhi. In the course of his conversation with

India's religious nobleman, Thurman asked Gandhi of his thoughts on the question of what the obstacle was that prevented America from spreading Christianity. Gandhi responded to Thurman's question by saying that the obstacle was that "Christianity as it is practiced, as it has been identified with Western culture, with Western civilization and colonialism. This is the greatest enemy that Jesus Christ has in my country—not Hinduism, or Buddhism, or any of the indigenous religions—but Christianity itself."[18] This statement of a pensive prophet set apart several thousand miles from the shining cities and the sylvan woodlands of America is nothing less than a sweeping condemnation of the brand of Christianity practiced here. It is a condemnatory word that strongly needs to be heeded and followed by radical corrective action. For while the Early Church of the Acts of the Apostles rose as a monolith of multiples in a world fractured and fragmented by rotten religion, polluted politics, and a crumbling culture, the contemporary church in America is warped and weak because of its racial rifts and cultural cleavages. The church at Antioch is an archetypal example of what it means to be a church of power in an upside down society. Empowered by the Spirit of God, she had the wisdom and audacity to have within her administrative and ecclesiastical staff men of the ebony hue to effect the decision that would send out into the world two of God's most powerful witnesses, Paul and Barnabas. The contemporary church in America has yet to measure up to this Biblical model; and as a result, it has relegated herself to the unenviable realm of dreaded weakness.

But we cannot end this discussion on a note of foul

---

[18]Howard Thurman, *With Head and Heart*. (New York: Harcourt Brace Jovanovich, 1979). p. 135.

gloom and blinding pessimism. Our study of the Acts of the Apostles tells us that there is reason and room for ambitious optimism. A last look at the Early Church of the Acts of the Apostles discloses that it rose up in the midst of a world mired in morbid morality, dying at the feet of decadent deities, enthralled by the threats of the throne in Rome, and a host of other horrors that strangled the very spirit. But the church flourished like a budding flower in the desert, a flower that strangely repelled the blistering heat of the sun and strongly resisted the parching breath of the desert wind and survived and thrived from a source of strength unseen by the human eye, a source that ran unhindered deep in the heart of the universe—God!

It would sound as it were a broken record if we were to reset the stage on which the Early Church acted out its magnificent drama of salvation's story. Suffice it to say that the situation was rough and the going was tough. The Early Church in no way was carried to the skies on flowery beds of ease. It marched through the flame and flood of persecution and suffering. But the more it marched and the more it suffered, the more it grew in phenomenal proportions. Luke is probably the most outstanding of the New Testament writers in the sense of picking up the importance of the Early Church's proliferation in spite of the pressures that afflicted it. He begins to tell us about this surge in the number of saints added to the church in chapter two of the Acts of the Apostles when he tells us that after Simon Peter's powerful sermon on the Day of Pentecost, ". . .they that gladly received his word were baptized; and the same day there were added unto them about three thousand souls" (Acts 2:41 KJV). He closes out this same chapter by indicating that there were still others added to the church; for he says, "And the Lord added to the church daily such as should be saved" (Acts 2:47b).

In chapter four, Luke begins by telling of the annoyance that was taking hold of the priests and captain of the temple and the Sadducees. Their annoyance was caused by the message of Jesus and His resurrection that raced through the city of Jerusalem from the mouths of the apostles. The logical thing for the temple authorities to do to silence these religious fanatics was to put them in prison. So they did! But it did no good; it only created a more conducive climate for more souls to be added to the church. Luke says that in spite of the imprisonment of the apostles, ". . .many of them which heard the word believed; and the number of the men was about five thousand" (Acts 4:4). In the following chapter, Luke continues to parade the proliferating church before us. Ananias and Sapphira failed the test of honesty in the church and the apostles gathered with the people in the portico of Solomon, and Luke says, "And believers were the more added to the Lord, multitudes both of men and women" (Acts 5:14). In chapter six when the ecclesiastical structure had been arranged for the church, Luke states that ". . .the word of God increased; and the number of the disciples multiplied in Jerusalem greatly; and a great company of the priests were obedient to the faith" (Acts 6:7).

In Samaria where racism was rife and prejudice for Jews had ossified, Philip, who was a Jew, who now followed Jesus, preached Christ, and it is said that ". . .the people with one accord gave heed unto those things which Philip spake . . . when they believed Philip preaching the things concerning the kingdom of God, and the name of Jesus Christ, they were baptized, both men and women" (Acts 8:6,12).

Paul's conversion on the Damascus Road gave Luke

the opportunity to speak of the swelling numbers of converts added to the church. The story is that one moment Paul was breathing out threats and murder against the disciples of the Lord (Acts 9:1). Obtaining permission from the officials of the temple to go to Damascus to seek out those of the Way, Paul set out on the road to Damascus. On that road, however, he met the Redemptive Force that changed his life forever. He was knocked to the ground and blinded so that he saw nothing, but heard only the voice of God challenging him and giving him new directions for his life. And so, rather than proceed on to Damascus to tear down the church, he went there to build it up for Christ. Escaping a plot on his life, Saul was delivered from the hands of Jews and went back to Jerusalem where he was received by the church as an apostle of the Lord. Luke used this setting to declare that, "Then had the churches rest throughout all Judea and Galilee and Samaria, and were edified; and walking in the fear of the Lord, and in the comfort of the Holy Ghost, were multiplied" (Acts 9:31).

In that same chapter nine, Luke quickly shifts to the miracles performed by Simon Peter in Lydda and Joppa. At Lydda, he healed a paralyzed and bedridden Aeneas; and at Joppa, he raised from the dead a disciple named Tabitha who had fallen sick and died. As a result of Peter's miraculous ministry in Joppa, Luke says,"And it was known throughout all Joppa, and many believed in the Lord" (Acts 9:42).

On the first missionary journey of Paul and Barnabas, as they took the Gospel into the land of Galatia, Luke discloses that the church experienced continued phenomenal growth. At Iconium, it is said that they entered the Jewish synagogue and preached so much so that ". . .a great multitude both of the Jews and also of the Greeks believed" (Acts 14:1). The beginning of the second missionary journey informs us of one of the sadder moments in the history of the Early Church, the separation of Paul and Barnabas. But in spite of this lamentable rift in relations, the church continued its tremendous growth. When Paul chose Silas to accompany him, the two went again to the land of Galatia. As they preached throughout the cities of Galatia, Luke says "...the churches [were] established in the faith, and increased in number daily" (Acts 16:5).

Such was the case as Paul and Silas went throughout Asia Minor preaching the Gospel. In spite of the suffering and tribulation they experienced, believers were added to the church. At Thessalonica, at Athens, at Corinth, and Ephesus, Paul and Silas suffered persecution and threats, but the church continued to flourish in numbers and strength.

There is little wonder why Luke continued to cite the phenomenal growth of the church of the Acts of the Apostles over and over again. This was to show that nothing could stand in the way of the marching phalanx of the church that was set in motion by the command of Jesus the Christ on the Mount of Olives side of the grave. Nothing! Nothing could stop the church because it was a movement empowered by the Spirit of God. Once the startled cluster of bewildered disciples had closed ranks with the addition of Matthias to replace Judas, and once they had come together and the Holy Spirit had sat upon them, nothing could stand in their way. As a monolith of multiples, they moved out and cured disease and maladies that afflicted the multitudes, overwhelmed demons, swept away false and pagan deities, set to flight rival religions, conquered racial prejudices, and overcame cultural cleavages. The Early Church of the Acts of the Apostles swept past every obstacle that stood in her path so much so that in spite of all of the contrived hindrances that were set before her, God continued to add members from day to day, such as should be saved. The church so overwhelmed her opposition that Luke closes out the story of the beginning of the church in the Acts of the Apostles by saying that in the Imperial City of Rome, Paul continued preaching the message of the Kingdom of God and teaching about Jesus Christ as Lord,   "...with all confidence, no man forbidding him" (Acts 28:31).

So there is no need for me to conclude this discussion of the movement of the church, whether then or now, on a note of foul gloom and blinding pessimism. Luke's story of the church of the Acts of the Apostles tells us that the church, whether then or now, is not an exercise in futility but is an instrument in the hands of God which crushes every evil thing in its path and is destined to stand in the victor's circle. This is enough to give us hope for the church today.

The hope for us is that God will once again empower the church with His Spirit and raise up witnesses for Himself who will be willing to suffer, and if need be, to die for the sake of His name—witnesses who will proclaim Christ as Lord of all the earth. God will empower the church so much so that she will march against the very gates of hell and the powers of death, and nothing shall prevail against her. She will crush every vestige of evil in her path. She will destroy every hindering obstacle and sweep past every standing opposition. She will be the very epitome of Joshua's battle axe that cuts its way through the wilderness of sin, of Jeremiah's hammer that breaks in pieces the rocks of oppression, of Daniel's stone hewn without hands out of the mountain, that rolled down through Babylon tearing down the kingdoms of iron, woodwork

and steel. But the movement of the church will not be of such that it will merely tear down; it will build up. For once it has overcome every evil and hindering cause, there shall gather of the saints a number from every nation that no man can number. They shall gather to stand in the victor's circle and God shall be in their midst. It shall be as John of the Revelation saw when he said:
> And I John saw the holy city, new Jerusalem, coming down from God out of heaven, prepared as a bride adorned for her husband. And I heard a great voice out of heaven saying, Behold, the tabernacle of God is with men, and He will dwell with them, and they shall be his people, and God himself shall be with them and be their God. And God shall wipe away all tears from their eyes; and there shall be no more death, neither sorrow, nor crying, neither shall there be any more pain: for the former things are passed away. (Rev. 21:2-4)

This was the hope of the Early Church of the Acts of the Apostles. She clung to that hope empowered by the Spirit of God. This is our hope today! What a magnificent thing it is to be a part of such a great movement, a movement that is destined to stand in the victor's circle with God.

Chapter V

THE CHURCH EMPOWERED BY GOD-ORDAINED ECCLESIASTICAL ORDER ACCORDING TO ACTS 6:1-7

INTRODUCTION

Throughout this book, I have tried to make the point that the nascent manifestation of the Christian Faith was as a church of power. The Early Church generated power because it prayed, witnessed, and strove diligently to move through its world in lock-step with one another, in harmony and union together. One of the reasons such harmony was possible was due to the unique understanding of the roles of individuals within the context of the church. Leaders in the church were known and understood to be such while others knew they were to be supportive and follow their leaders. The New Testament's references to bishops and deacons make it evident there was ecclesiastical order within the church. We see this very early in the church with Paul's greetings to the "bishops and deacons" at Philippi (*see*, Phil. 1:1). The Acts 6:1-7 account of the selection of deacons for the Early Church reflects a growing need for men within the ecclesiastical community who could assist the apostles in those things which were less than spiritual. The clear delineation of requirements for bishops and deacons in I Timothy 3:1-13 makes it obvious that church order was in effect and that qualifications for each were to be stringently met. The point here is this, as the Early Church grew, ecclesiastical order became a must. Moreover, the Early Church saw her responsibility of clearly spelling out the levels of responsibility and the things for which each level was responsible.

This is not to say there was no internal struggle between personalities and levels of authority within the New Testament church. There was! In the Acts of the Apostles itself, there was serious contention between Paul and Barnabas over the question of the feasibility of taking John Mark on the Second Missionary Journey. Paul adjudged that he should not be taken. This led to a split between him and Barnabas. This is one of the saddest moments in the development of the Early Church. In addition, some theologians surmise that the two separate sections in the Acts of the Apostles, one for Peter and one for Paul, is reflective of a schism within the Early Church between the two camps. However, II Peter 3:15 seems to show that this is not true (especially with Peter's reference to "...our beloved brother Paul"). Finally, the fact that there is no reference to Paul the Apostle in the Revelation to John (there is only a reference to the twelve apostles) has caused some to draw the conclusion that there was friction within the Early Church.

These speculations do not dismiss the fact that the Early Church strove with all it had to pursue unity and harmony to the end that it would manifest itself in power to a sinful world. In the Acts of the Apostles, we have a statement about the developing Early Church manifesting itself in many ways as a church of power. In the sixth chapter of the Acts of the Apostles, we see another reason this was true, viz., because it followed

God-ordained ecclesiastical order. There is much the Black church can learn as she tries to solve one of her most serious problems.

THE PROBLEM

One of the phenomena which has reduced many Black Baptist churches to a state of impotence in a spiritual, social, and political sense is the administrative strain that has occurred in the relationship between the pastor and deacons. Most Black Baptist churches have what is called a "Deacon Board." (In the African Methodist Episcopal Church the sequel is called a Board of Stewards.) Generally, this is a group of men who have been recommended and/or selected by the congregation and ordained by the church's pastor and a panel of other pastors and, in some cases, laymen. In contrast to desirability, in so many cases, there is not a harmonious relationship between the pastor and deacon board. In too many cases, deacon boards assert authority over the pastor so much so that they often are at loggerheads with one another and can accomplish nothing for the good of the congregation.

A strange phenomenon has occurred in the Black Baptist church as it relates to deacons. There is a philosophy that says deacons are the ones who "tell the pastor what to do." Some of them have been known to say, "We hired you, brother pastor, and we tell you what to do!" For some peculiar and unknown reason, many deacons in the Black church have a mind to think they are the ones who "run the church"!

That the "Official Board of Deacons," as this entity has come to be known, conceptually strives to run the church has been manifested in many and sundry ways across the nation. Tales are many, sordid, and sinister of how deacon boards have seized power from pastors. In some instances, they have surreptitiously called meetings of the congregation for the purpose of voting out the pastor. Mental pain and spiritual anguish have been the lot of many a pastor of Black Baptist churches because of action taken by the "Official Board of Deacons." Moreover, in many instances, the church has been reduced to impotence and a mass of inert spiritual matter because of power plays and political ploys of the "Official Board of Deacons." Many a head has been bowed in shame because of a painful ecclesiastical coup d'etat by the "Official Board of Deacons," removing a long-standing pastor from his post, leaving the congregation without leadership or a sense of direction.

The origin of this peculiar ecclesiastical arrangement certainly does not emerge out of the Bible. The arrangement of the deacon being "the" leader in the church comes from the larger White church culture. At one of the conferences of Christian educators held each December at the Sunday School Publishing Board, NBC, USA, Inc., in Nashville, Tennessee, Dr. Riggins R. Earl, Jr., read a document from a White church community obtained from the Library of Congress in Washington, D.C., which provided an eyewitness account of the prescribed, prearranged relationship between pastors and deacons in the rural Black church in American Slavery in the South.

Dr. Earl read of how the church was designed to accommodate an itinerant Black preacher, who would come to preach on a given Sunday, and a head deacon who lived among the people and was in charge of the religious life of the people who attended the church. The document seemed to have been written by a White person, maybe the plantation slave master. It proceeded to denigrate the Black preacher who came from afar; for example, in Mississippi, the preacher may have come out of Memphis or Jackson, Tennessee, Laurel or Hattiesburg, Mississippi.

The Black preacher, it was exclaimed, was a womanizer and one who imbibed alcohol. He was one smitten with moral turpitude. On the other hand, the deacons were highly moral men, family men, and residents of the community. They were the ones who had the welfare of the church at heart and indeed contended for the welfare of the members of the church; and, thus, by virtue of this position "the" true leaders of the community.

The document read by Dr. Earl unilaterally placed the political power of the church squarely in the hands of the deacons. Herein is a clear historical description of how disparity and contention were built into the relationship of the pastor and deacons in the Black Baptist church during the time of slavery in America's Southland. In no way does this development conform with the Biblical description of the relationship of the pastor and deacons in the Black Baptist church.

Fundamentally, Negro Baptists have adopted a "board" system from the White Southern Baptist church. White Baptists, Southern and maybe Northern (or American), apparently have adopted a "board" system from some nebular region of American society. Such an arrangement has as a structure a board of directors composed of a chairman of the board and board members. All decisions are made by and through the "board." The white Baptist church, which operates more or less as a profit-making business, operates on the basis of "official boards," with an official chairman. This board arrangement is extremely powerful. The "pastor" most often is only titular and has no power or authority to make significant church business decisions. His responsibility is that of preaching, and that according to the likes and dislikes of the "board" and church membership. The "democratic" process, the driving force of the corporate "board" arrangement, is the same driving force within the church with the Official Board of Deacons as the entity which wields its power. There is little difference between the "board" arrangement in corporate America and the "board" arrangement for the White church.

The question of the origin of this "board" arrangement, when it comes to the church, is very interesting and begs a response. The response to this question can locate in history the origin of a very serious problem in the Black Baptist church. If we can locate the origin of this phenomenon, we will attempt to counter and obliterate it by looking seriously at Biblical models and mandates as it relates to the relationship of the pastor and deacons in the Black Baptist church.

One response comes from Edward T. Hiscox's *Principles and Practices for Baptist Churches.* This manual was first published in 1894 as *The New Directory for Baptist Churches*, by Kregel Publications in Grand Rapids, Michigan. Dr. Hiscox, an American (or Northern) Baptist, wrote this work as a guiding principle primarily for Baptists of the North. It has always carried great currency in all of the United States, including many pastors and churchmen of the National Baptist Convention, USA, Inc. As it relates to the place of deacons and a "Board of Deacons," he does have something rather profound to say.

In chapter four, which is devoted to "church officers," Dr. Hiscox gives his position on the subject:

> Deacons should be watchfull guardians of the purity and good order of the churches, striving to maintain a healthful tone of piety and Christian activity in the body. But they do not constitute a coordinate branch for the administration of its government, and in the exercise of their functions must act only in conjunction with the pastor, not independent of him; <u>except</u> in very

rare and urgent cases. Hence, while it is desirable for the pastor to have meetings with his deacons often or statedly for consultation and advice, it is not proper for them to hold meetings as a "board of deacons," independent of and without the advice of the pastor, as sometimes is done.[19]

Hiscox does not give any indication of the origination of the term "board of deacons," although he makes reference to it. His reference, ". . .as sometimes is done," is a veiled allusion to something that already is aloft and in place somewhere and with significant influence in the church. However, he clearly states that this arrangement does not have a place in the church. He gives a clear delineation of the responsibility of deacons in their relationship with the pastor. He also instructs that deacons are not to "hold meetings as a 'board of deacons'" independent of the pastor. This rather poignant treatment of the subject seems to get at something that had been causing serious problems for the Baptist church. Dr. Hiscox, an American Baptist, insists that the cause of the problem is not Biblical and prescribes remedy for the same. Surely, he was on the right course.

In contrast to Dr. Hiscox's position, when we peruse the plethora of material coming out of the Southern Baptist camp concerning deacons, we find heavy emphasis on the concept of "boards of deacons." Charles W. Deweese's book of 1979 on the emerging role of deacons cited deacon boards as one of the phenomena which caused controversy and problems for Southern Baptist churches. Deweese concluded that Southern Baptists made use of deacons in the nineteenth century as businessmen, operating the business affairs of the church.

---

[19]Edward T. Hiscox, *Principles and Practices for Baptist Churches*. (Grand Rapids: Kregel Publications), p. 115.

However, as they moved into the twentieth century, Southern Baptists moved more toward utilizing deacons in wider areas of ministry, in addition to the business matters. Today, as Deweese sees it, Southern Baptists are including women in the new emerging role for deacons.[20]

Howard B. Foshee is such an authority on the Baptist church that Southern Baptists have utilized his services to develop a 1973 church manual.[21] Also, he has authored a book primarily dealing with deacons from a Southern Baptist perspective.[22] In the *Broadman Church Manual*, Foshee expresses a reaction to what he calls "the unfortunate phrase 'board of deacons.'" He expresses this in the course of citing the early development (1700's and 1800's) of deacons being assigned administrative work in the church. He observes that:

> Gradually deacons were called on to handle more of the administrative work of the church. Oftentimes the deacons were the only elected church officers available to care for finances and property.[23]

This "concept of a legislative board" is what he calls "unfortunate." What he posits as the modus operandi for the administration of the affairs of the church is:

> Only the congregation, under the leadership of the Holy Spirit, should make major decisions for the church.[24]

From this postulation, Foshee concludes that councils and committees should be formed from members within the congregation to take care of the "business" of the church in its totality. As he describes his process, the

---

[20] Charles W. Deweese, *The Emerging Role of Deacons*. (Nashville, Tennessee: Broadman Press, 1979), pp. 59f.
[21] Howard B. Foshee, *Broadman Church Manual*. (Nashville, Tennessee: Broadman Press, 1973).
[22] *See, The Ministry of the Deacon*. (Nashville, Tennessee: Broadman Press).
[23] Howard B. Foshee, *Broadman Church Manual*. (Nashville, Tennessee: Broadman Press, 1973), p. 102.
[24] Op. cit., p. 103.

pastor is only a partner, not the leader, in this process. As for deacons, their realm of responsibility is that of lay preaching, caring for the church membership, and engagement in a deacons' family ministry program. In none of this, however, in Foshee's conception, is the pastor involved as having any authority. He merely is a participant. In attempting to avoid the damaging concept of deacons who have unilateral administrative responsibility and authority, Foshee's formula still comes far short of what Acts 6:1ff., offers the church of power.

Robert E. Naylor is one of many Southern Baptists who sees the deacons' role as administrative in nature with little or no responsibility to the pastor. As for becoming a deacon, Naylor states that it is a matter of "democratic" judgment on the part of the church congregation. Incidentally, he says consultation with the pastor is suggested before such a judgment is made.[25]

In this arrangement, the function of deacons is purely administrative, accompanied by the adornments of power and authority. Deacons must place "deacons' meeting" before anything else. The chairman, a deacon, is the presiding officer at the deacons' meeting, not the pastor. Essentially, these are the ones who care for the business of the church, and that as a deacon board.

As we look farther back into the history of Southern Baptists' approach to the relationship between the pastor and deacons in the church, we begin to detect the origin of such confusion. For example, in 1966, Southern Baptists celebrated the sixth printing of J. M. Pendleton's book, *Baptist Church Manual*. Pendleton represents Southern Baptists' position on deacons which goes back as far as

---

[25]Robert E. Naylor, *The Baptist Deacon*. (Nashville, Tennessee: Broadman Press, 1955), pp. 34ff.

the 1860's, when this publication was initially printed. Pendleton struggles to remain faithful to the Biblical understanding of deacons. However, he eventually concedes to the pressures of modern-day living in America with its corporate mentality. For example, the pastor is an "employee" of the church. Hence, although deacons could be a part of the oversight of the pastor's duties, Pendleton recommends that a church personnel committee be set in place. This committee would be responsible for developing personnel policies and procedures "...for all *employees*, including the pastor" (emphasis mine). The pastor being the "employee" of the church, the deacon(s) then, as members of the church personnel committee, would be the "boss" of the pastor, to tell him what to do. This, then, is a tacit concession to the "board" arrangement, although there is no reference to such, either pro or con. Such political posturing of deacons to "tell the pastor what to do" is probably where Black men serving as deacons in the Black Baptist church got such a notion.[26]

With the invaluable assistance of Charles W. Deweese, we probably have located the origin of the concept of deacons constituting an "official board" of the church in R. B. C. Howell. A pastor of the First Baptist Church in Nashville, Tennessee, Howell authored a book in 1846 entitled *The Deaconship* (Philadelphia: American Baptist Publication Society, 1846). In this publication, the Nashville pastor spoke of deacons as the "financial officers of the church." In addition, he assigned a title to them as a "Board of Officers." The responsibility assigned to such men was that of the management of church business and the placement of all church property and monies under

---

[26]J. M. Pendeleton, *Baptist Church Manual*. (Nashville, Tennessee: Broadman Press, 1966), pp. 29-35.

their supervision.[27] Indeed, herein lies the origin of the concept of the "official board of deacons" with unlimited authority. Inquiry discloses that Howell's book has been widely used in National Baptist churches. Its Baptist polity and practice have been widely adhered to in Black Baptist churches. It has been this concept, adopted without question by Black Baptist churches, which has been a demonic nemesis, rending congregations apart and eternally dividing pastors and deacons.

The question is, how do we correct this grave situation? Where do we turn? Our rejoinder is, to the Bible and its dramatic unfolding story of a church of power propelled by God-ordained ecclesiastical order.

WHAT DOES THE BIBLE SAY?

One of the great errors we as Blacks have made in our pursuit of the acceptable manner in which the administrative arrangement of the church is set up is that we have looked to the models of the larger culture as our example. What we have seen above is indicative of that fact. Moreover, the Black church has depended heavily on the theology and ecclesiology of the larger culture for understanding what the Bible says about a particular subject. In that respect, we have been the recipients of error-ridden and flawed theology and ecclesiology.

Surely, it must be said that we as a people were introduced to the Christian Faith by the larger culture. Indeed, it also must be said that the manner in which we were introduced to the Christian Faith was in no way to benefit The Faith itself, but to use it to enslave a whole race of people and make them more docile in their servitude. But though stony the road we have trod and

---

[27]R. B. C. Howell, *The Deaconship*. (Philadelphia: American Baptist Publication Society, 1846).

bitter the chastening rod, we must acknowledge that the Christian Faith came by means of our former slave masters. There must be some salvific reason for this in the plan of God. In such a condition, one is driven to assume the attitude of the Apostle Paul when he says,

> Some indeed preach Christ even of envy and strife; and some also of good will: The one preach Christ of contention, not sincerely, supposing to add affliction to my bonds: But the other of love, knowing that I am set for the defence of the gospel. What then? notwithstanding, every way, whether in pretence, or in truth, Christ is preached; and I therein do rejoice, yea, and will rejoice. (Phil. 1:15-18)

Though the Christian Faith was introduced to Black people in order to increase our bonds, yet we rejoice that Christ was then and is now being preached.

Having said that, however, we are driven still to try and untangle the theological imbroglio and ecclesiological obfuscation which has wreaked havoc in the Black Baptist church. From the time of American Slavery, Blacks have been exposed to quite a distorted version of Christianity. It is our position that this is what has happened as it relates to the problem of conflict in the Black church between the pastor and deacons. What is being said here is that many of the problems encountered in the Black Baptist church can be attributed to the flawed theology, ecclesiology, Christian education and training shared with it, or imposed upon it, by the White church.

In this discussion, we will examine some of the ways this has happened. Once we will have completed this task, we will look at the Scriptures themselves for the answer we seek. We will make use of three commentaries which represent the church of the larger culture. One of the works is a respectable publication by the German New

Testament scholar, Ernst Haenchen. This commentary on *The Acts of the Apostles* was first published in Germany subsequent to Haenchen's initial work in 1946. We will work with the English version which was translated and has a copyright of 1971. The next commentary will be *The Acts of the Apostles*, 1931, edited by F. J. Foakes Jackson and Kirsopp Lake. These scholars represent moderate to liberal scholarship, both Continental (German) and English. The third will be Volume 9 of *The Interpreter's Bible, The Acts*, by G. H. C. MacGregor. This is the commentary of the United Methodist Church of the United States of America and is used extensively by a large segment of pastors and preachers of the Black church. For balance, I will interject my translation of the Greek text of Acts 6:1-7 as well as my understanding of the theological meaning of the same. In fact, this is how we will conclude this chapter.

CHURCH GROWTH AS THE NEED FOR PASTORAL ASSISTANCE IN ACTS 6:1-7

The text which gives us the historical origination of the deacon in the New Testament is very interesting indeed. (Admittedly, the first reference to deacons in the New Testament is by the Apostle Paul in his letter to the Philippians, 1:1.) Acts 6:1ff., is the setting. At the outset, we are told that the Early Church experienced phenomenal growth. Luke makes an impassioned effort to stress the growth of the Early Church, cf., Acts 1:8; 2:41, 47; 4:4, possibly 4:32f.; and 5:14. By the time of chapter six, a great strain was placed upon the leadership of the church. The sheer numbers themselves were overwhelming to the apostles who provided leadership for the congregation. Three thousand alone were added when Peter preached his great sermon. Five thousand are cited in Acts 4:4. These numbers are staggering. Obviously, assistance was needed.

In the midst of the growing numbers of believers in the church, neglect of one segment of the membership (the Hellenist widows) developed and caused a rumble and disturbance to erupt. The Hellenists began to complain that their widows were neglected over against the Hebrew widows in the distribution of the daily provisions. Haenchen does not think Luke (the writer of The Acts of the Apostles) is necessarily interested in who is responsible for the disparity, confusion, and disagreement between the Hellenist widows and Hebrew widows.

The Interpreter's Bible does not address the matter of the cause of the problem between the Hebrew and Hellenist widows. It does cite the fact that widows without legal protection were a difficult problem for the Early Church. It was one, according to *The Interpreter's Bible*, which had to be dealt with. According to this commentary, the problem was solved by the Early Church's adoption of the Jewish custom of providing relief.

Foakes-Jackson and Kirsopp Lake do not entertain the matter at all. However, there is a problem in the Early Church—one which had to be dealt with in order to maintain the strength of the church. Regardless of the cause of the problem, it had to be dealt with. Our interest is to determine how the problem was dealt with and how such resolution instructs the Black church in our time in terms of proper ecclesiastical arrangement and relationship between the pastor and deacons.

The basic economic operation of the Early Church is described earlier in the Acts. As early as chapter two, it is stated that every member sold their possessions and pooled their resources for the common good of the total membership. Acts 2:44f., gives the example of what was done in this regard, i.e., pooling resources for the common good of the membership; however, there is no indication of how it was done. The text simply says that after the possessions and goods of the membership were sold, they "...parted them to all men as every man had need" (Acts 2:45b).

This socialistic approach to ecclesiastical life, a communal lifestyle if you will, was continued in chapter four of the Acts. There, oneness of soul and heart is stressed (cf., Acts 4:32) and having all things in common becomes even the more prominent. One peculiarity here is that emphasis is placed on the fact that no member of the church had need for anything. Members of the Early Church sold their possessions and brought the proceeds to the Apostles who equally distributed them to all. However, there yet is not given an idea of the procedure by which this was done. The text simply says:

> Neither was there any among them that lacked: for as many as were possessors of lands or houses sold them, and brought the prices of the things that were sold, And laid them down at the apostles' feet: and distribution was made unto every man according as he had need. (Acts 4:34f.)

Here, the indication is that the apostles held the responsibility of distributing the proceeds which were laid at their feet by the members of the congregation. This is, however, where the problem entered in. With the ever-increasing numbers within the membership of the Early Church and the concomitant responsibility of taking care of them, the apostles saw the need to secure assistance. This indeed is the setting of chapter six and the prelude for the need for assistants who subsequently would be called "deacons."

It is important to note that nowhere in Acts 6:1-7 is the term deacon (δ ι ά κ ο ν ο ς=*diakonos*) used. In Acts 6:1ff., the term διακονία =*diakonia*, ministry or ministration does appear, cf., ἐν τῇ διακονίᾳ τῇ καθημερινῇ = "daily ministration." The infinitive form of the word is used in verse two when the apostles assert that they should not leave the Word of God to "serve tables," cf., διακονεῖν τραπέζαις = *diakonein trapezais*. The term for "deacon" is not used in the text itself, but the situation in which such an one was to serve dictates the term, i.e., διάκονος = *diakonos*.

SELECTION OF THE FIRST DEACONS OF THE EARLY CHURCH

Now that we know the situation which brought about deacons in the New Testament, the question comes, how were they selected? What was their relationship to the apostles? The answer to these questions begins in verse two of chapter six of The Acts.

"The Twelve" or the apostles, as it were, those who represent the pastor(s) in our contemporary church, called the congregation together. It is important to note the sequence of things. The apostles called together the members of the church. The members of the church did not call the meeting:

> Then the twelve called the multitude of the disciples unto them. . . . (Acts 6:2).

The force of the word used here, προσκαλεσάμενοι = *proskalesamenoi*, is that of the disciples calling to themselves the multitude, the membership of the Early Church of the Acts of the Apostles. In effect, they summoned them to a meeting to deal with a serious problem. In no way can the text be read to mean that the membership, the multitude, called a meeting of themselves or that they convened a meeting of the congregation. Clearly, it is the apostles who do this. In doing so, the apostles demonstrate leadership which was appropriate for pastors of the Early Church. Such process was vigorously taken up by subsequent apostles, e.g., Paul, Peter, the writer to the Hebrews, John, and Timothy, who was urged by Paul to assume such style of leadership.

This procedure flies in the face of contemporary church life in so many instances. Following after the church of the larger culture, which itself follows the corporate mentality of boards, the Black Baptist church concedes to the temptation of lay members calling a meeting of church members without the knowledge or approval of the pastor. Often, it is the "board of deacons" or "board of trustees" which calls such a meeting. It has come to pass that such meetings are often called for the express purpose of voting the pastor out of the church. In Acts 6:2, it is the apostles who call the multitude of the congregation to a meeting to deal with a critical situation.

THE APOSTLES' REQUEST FOR ASSISTANCE

Once the apostles had summoned the multitude, they laid out the reason for their request for assistance. The latter part of verse two of chapter six discloses their rationale for asking for help in the crisis within the fellowship. Οὐκ ἀρεστόν ἐστιν =*Ouk areston estin* should be translated "It is not right" or "pleasing" to leave the Word of God and διακονεῖν τραπέζαις = *diakonein trapezais*, i.e., "to minister to the tables," or "to serve food."

The force of this statement is unusual and remarkable. Of significance is that the membership of the koinonia (fellowship-congregation) did not come forth with the suggestion that the apostles, the preachers, needed help. A great deal is said here, e.g., the congregation's inability to see the proclamation of the gospel and the study of the Word of God as paramount for the church. It is the apostles who conclude that the proclamation of the gospel and the study of the Word of God take precedence over any and all other kinds of activity within the fellowship (cf., Luke 10:38-42).

Of a truth, it is the position of the New Testament that the preacher, pastor, the apostle is the leader of the congregation of believers in Jesus Christ. It was the pastor, preacher, or apostle, whichever is preferred, to whom Jesus gave the keys to the Kingdom:

> And I will give unto thee the keys of the kingdom of heaven: and whatsoever thou shalt bind on earth shall be bound in heaven; and whatsoever thou shalt loose on earth shall be loosed in heaven. (Matt. 16:19)

It is the pastor, preacher, disciple, or apostle to whom Jesus speaks and bequeaths unique insight into the wisdom of God:

> Therefore every scribe which is instructed unto the kingdom of heaven, is like unto a man that is an householder, which bringeth forth out of the treasure things new and old. (Matt. 13:52)

It is the pastor, preacher, apostle to whom Jesus gave extraordinary powers:

> And when he had called unto him his twelve disciples, he gave them power against unclean spirits, to cast them out, and to heal all manner of sickness and all manner of disease. (Matt. 10:1)

It is clear here that it is with authority that the apostles speak in making their request for assistance. This is the authority given them by Jesus ($\dot{\epsilon}\xi o\upsilon\sigma\iota\alpha$ = *exousia*), cf. Mt. 28:18. It is authority which they are spiritually bound to exercise and command respect, cf., Gal. 1:8f. However it is not authority which they are obliged to share with anyone else. Hence, in this case, the apostles are simply requesting assistance in the work, not relief from responsibility for the work nor of sharing a portion of their apostolic authority with anyone else.

With apostolic authority, the leaders of the Early Church of Acts 6 gave the congregation the directions as to what they were to do to alleviate the situation created by the complaint of the Hellenist widows against the Hebrew widows. "Wherefore brethren," is how the directive begins, "look ye out among you," ἐπισκέψασθε = *episkepsasthe*. (Note: It is interesting that the term used in the apostles' expression is ἐπισκέψασθε = *episkepsasthe*, a similar term which is descriptive of the apostles' later title in the church, viz., ἐπίσκοπος = *episkopos* = bishop, cf., Phil. 1:1; 1 Tim. 3:1f. What is being suggested here, if anything, is not clear, e.g., whether there was a transference of apostolic authority to "oversee" this part of the work of the church. This could be true, and yet there could be no significance to it at all.) Essentially, the preachers instructed the multitude to look out over the congregation and select men who would take the responsibility of "waiting tables" (τραπέζαις = *trapezais*). Waiting tables could be a reference to the dining table, or, more than likely, it could mean more or less taking care of the money changer's table, i.e., the table which represents the bank of the Early Church community.

Thus, the directions given were, "...look ye out among you seven men of honest report, full of the Holy Ghost and wisdom, whom we may appoint over this business." The questions which leap out here are myriad. Are the apostles directing the multitude, i.e., the congregation, to choose the seven with the appropriate credentials and then set them over the work of serving tables? Is this a congregational matter? Are those who were to come to be known as "deacons" to be chosen by and serve at the whim of the congregation? Or, was the congregation to be the conduit through which the authority of the Apostles would take effect? Would the congregation choose the seven, according to the guidelines laid out by the Apostles? Would they then bring them to the Apostles for sanction and approval. These are the questions with which communions and congregations of the contemporary genre have wrestled, oftentimes arriving at the painfully wrong conclusion which has led to powerful deacon boards which have wreaked havoc with the pastor and deacons within the congregation.

MISGUIDANCE OF CONTEMPORARY COMMENTARIES

In addition to misguidance in the Black church by consulting with errant church administration manuals from the larger church community, as has been discussed above, wrong conclusions in the Black church are also too often drawn after consulting with commentaries produced by the theologians of the church of the larger culture. This is likely to be the case in the Black church's interpretation of Acts 6:1-7.

When we inquire of the commentaries we have consulted for this excursus, we discover the kinds of theological conclusions which have fostered confusion and division within the Black church. For example, in response to the question of who exercised authority in Acts 6:2f., in the selection of the seven "disciples," Haenchen clearly states that it was not the Apostles who demonstrated their apostolic authority in the selection of the seven. He concedes that it is "the twelve [who] call an assembly of the whole community" to announce that it is not right or pleasing to God that the preachers, apostles, should leave the Word of God to wait on tables. Haenchen does not wish to risk taking sides with the apostles in the matter. He states, in a very uncertain manner, ". . .the apostles are not stipulating but suggesting" what should be done to resolve the problem. Alarmingly, Haenchen concludes that "...it is the community which decides." Democracy is indeed functional in the Early Church of the Acts of the Apostles, as far as Haenchen is concerned. In contrast to this notion, the Early Church of the Acts of the Apostles lived under a theocracy, just as the children of Israel in the Old Testament. The only interest the apostles had in the matter, according to Haenchen, is that "Luke is rather explaining to the reader why the Apostles did not themselves assume this responsibility."[28]

Foakes-Jackson and Lake do not help us very much either. Our dilemma remains. Momentarily, they flirt with the possibility of the choice of the seven being that of the apostles. As it relates to the meaning of verse three of chapter six they say:

> If it is right and is pressed [i.e., the text of the "B" text, *Vaticanus*] it means that the choice of the Seven was made by the apostles, while the text of ℵ A C and the Western authorities means that the choice was left to the congregation. Even, however, with the text of B it is possible that the "we" means the whole Church rather than the apostles only.[29]

The problem here is that Foakes-Jackson and Lake do not wish to make a decision. The conclusion of, not who chose the Seven but, who was in charge during this crucial time is left to the individual or the church body themselves. This commentary is not much help at all.

G. H. C. MacGregor's treatment of this text in *The Interpreter's Bible Commentary* demonstrates a similar kind of hesitance and trepidation at seeing the Apostles

---

[28]Ernst Haenchen, Bernard Noble, tr. *The Acts of the Apostles, A Commentary*. (Philadelphia: Westminster Press, 1971), p. 262.
[29]F. J. Foakes Jackson and Kirsopp Lake, eds. *The Acts of the Apostles*. Volume 4. (Philadelphia: Westminster Press), p. 65.

as entirely in charge.
> Pick out from among you: It is the congregation which makes the selection, while the apostles set them apart. Curiously Codex Vaticanus (B) reads, "Let us choose, brethren, seven men from among you." Which may imply, though not necessarily, that the apostles made the selection also.[30]

It should be noted that the *Interpreter's Bible Commentary* is widely used by many contemporary Black pastors and preachers who have the awesome responsibility of leading a congregation of God's people who happen to be Black. Reading this commentary, along with Haenchen and Foakes-Jackson and Lake, would render them completely confused. For one thing, these commentaries speak freely of various codices, e.g., "Vaticanus" as does the *Interpreter's Bible Commentary* above. Most Black pastors and preachers do not have a working knowledge of the various texts from which scholars have drawn to make interpretations of the Biblical text. Most Black pastors and preachers have not had divinity school or seminary training which exposes them to this kind of discipline. Why this is the case is altogether another question, one into which someone must subsequently inquire, but we do not have that opportunity at this time. It can be said, however, that in 1933, Carter G. Woodson intimated in his *Miseducation of the Negro* that "The Traducer," his surrogate name for the White oppressor, discouraged Blacks from pursuing education in any and every field, including theology and pastoral concerns. The traducer insisted that with the Negro's natural ability, e.g., to preach, he did not need education.

---

[30]G. H. C. MacGregor. *The Acts of the Apostles.* Volume 9 of *The Interpreter's Bible.* (Nashville, Tennessee: Abingdon Press, 1954), p. 89.

What Black preachers have, however, is the Bible, the King James Version for the most part. The King James Version of the Bible is a distillation of the sixty-six books which were formally accepted by the church in A.D. 325. This version of the Bible surely has flaws in various word translations (e.g., where it often translates "δοῦλος = *doulos*" to mean "servant" rather than "slave," as the term always is translated to mean. See Kittel's *Word Book of the New Testament* and Fein, Behn, and Kümmel's *Greek Lexicon*). However, the King James Version of the Bible is as good a translation as any other in terms of faithfully transmitting the Biblical tradition. Where the problem enters in is with the theological and ecclesiological interpretation of the Bible by White theologians and preachers. These may confuse those who are influenced by listening to them preach or reading their commentaries. Those who write commentaries are privy, to some extent, to the plethora of ancient manuscripts which surfaced during the time of and following the formal acceptance of the sixty-six book corpus in ca. A.D. 325. What may help Blacks combat the confusion that emanates from the White theological camp is to engage in biblical/theological study themselves. However, even with this, there is the need to master knowledge of the Bible itself.

What this leads to is the question of how we understand the Bible itself. Dr. Leander Keck, former New Testament professor at Vanderbilt Divinity School and former Dean of the Divinity School at Yale University, always emphasized to his classes at Vanderbilt that "There is no better commentary on the Bible than the Bible itself." This writer has always taken that statement seriously. Let us, then, look at the Bible as commentary on the passage in question.

THE BIBLE AS COMMENTARY:
THE OLD TESTAMENT PRECEDENT TO ACTS 6

In Exodus 18:13ff., there is a sequel to Acts 6:1-7. This is one of the Old Testament passages which should be looked at when attempting to theologically understand Acts 6:1-7. Subsequently, the understanding gleaned from the study should be applied to the contemporary Black church. It may be well to set out the entire passage before attempting to peel from it the layers of meaning there are for the Black church today:

> And it came to pass on the morrow, that Moses sat to judge the people: and the people stood by Moses from the morning unto the evening. And when Moses' father in law saw all that he did to the people, he said, What is this thing that thou doest to the people? why sittest thou thyself alone, and all the people stand by thee from morning unto even? And Moses said unto his father in law, Because the people come unto me to inquire of God: When they have a matter, they come unto me; and I judge between one another, and I do make them know the statutes of God, and his laws. And Moses' father in law said unto him, The thing that thou doest is not good. Thou wilt surely wear away, both thou, and this people that is with thee: for this thing is too heavy for thee; thou art not able to perform it thyself alone. Hearken now unto my voice, I will give thee counsel, and God shall be with thee: Be thou for the people to God-ward, that thou mayest bring the causes unto God: And thou shalt teach them ordinances and laws, and shalt shew them the way wherein they must walk, and the work that they must do. Moreover thou shalt provide out of all the people able men, such as fear God, men of truth, hating covetousness; and place such over them, to be rulers of thousands, and rulers of hundreds, rulers of fifties, and rulers of tens. And let them judge the people at all seasons: and it

shall be, that every great matter they shall bring unto thee, but every small matter they shall judge: so shall it be easier for thyself, and they shall bear the burden with thee. If thou shalt do this thing, and God command thee so, then thou shalt be able to endure, and all this people shall also go to their place in peace. (Exodus 18:13-23).

In a similar way to that of Acts 6, the press of work was becoming too much for the leader Moses. He sat to judge the people of Israel from morning to evening. Moses' father-in-law Jethro became concerned for his well-being and encouraged him to seek assistance. Although Moses sincerely sought to judge between the members of the congregation to make them to know the statutes of God (cf., Ex. 18:16), Jethro was afraid his son-in-law would wear out himself and the people as well (ibid., v. 18). It is important to note that Jethro spoke not on his own behalf but that of God, cf., Exodus 18:19, ". . .I will give thee counsel, and God shall be with thee." Jethro was a priest of the Most High God, the priest of Midian. Thus, his interest was that of the interests of God.

The specific instructions Jethro gave to Moses were very similar to those given to the multitude in Acts. He instructed Moses to choose the following type of men to assist him with smaller and insignificant matters:

1. Able men
2. Men of truth
3. Such as fear God
4. Hating covetousness

These were to be placed over segments of the people, rulers of thousands, hundreds, fifties, and tens to have authority over small and insignificant matters.

Every great matter, however, was to be brought to Moses (cf., Ex. 18:22). The Lord placed on Jethro's heart the importance of the "welfare of Moses and the people" (cf., Ex. 18:7; 22, 23). If Moses is faithful to these guidelines, ". . . thou shalt be able to endure, and all this people shall also go to their place in peace" (Ex. 18:23). It is important to note that none of this is Jethro's doing. He does not initiate these instructions on his own authority. He is driven to say that "God command thee so," i.e., to execute what has been given by way of fatherly advice, then ". . .thou shalt be able to endure, and all this people shall also go to their place in peace." The record is that "Moses hearkened to the voice of his father-in-law, and did all that he had said" (v. 24). Acts 6 cannot be understood without a clear understanding of Exodus 18:13-23.

It further stands to reason that Acts 6:1-7 is understood best in light of Numbers 11:16-17, 24-25. Moreover, this passage must be linked with the aforementioned passage, Exodus 18:13-23. The situation in Numbers 11:16-17 is very similar to Exodus 18:13-23 in that the work of leading the children of Israel was overwhelming to Moses. Moses requested assistance from God. God's response was a directive to select seventy men of the elders of the congregation. These were to bear the burden of the people as a way of giving relief to Moses. However, one significant dimension in this process was that God would take Moses' spirit and give it to the elders selected to assist him:

> And the Lord said unto Moses, Gather unto me seventy men of the elders of Israel, whom thou knowest to be the elders of the people, and officers over them; and bring them unto the tabernacle of the congregation, that they may stand there with thee.
>
> And I will come down and talk with thee there: and I will take of the spirit which is upon thee, and will put it upon them; and they shall bear the burden of the people with thee, that thou bear it not thyself alone.

> And Moses went out, and told the people the words of the Lord, and gathered the seventy men of the elders of the people, and set them round about the tabernacle.
>
> And the Lord came down in a cloud, and spake unto him and took of the spirit that was upon him, and gave it unto the seventy elders: and it came to pass, that, when the spirit rested upon them, they prophesied, and did not cease. (Numbers 11:16-17; 24-25)

There are some striking occurrences here. Of importance is what we do not read. We do not read of a board of officers which will help Moses. We do read of the seventy men as "elders of the people and officers over them" (Numbers 11:16). We do not read of, however, a "board" as the operational structure. Hence, we do not read of a "chairman of the board." We do read that God took the spirit that was upon Moses and gave it to the seventy elders. Their empowerment came as a result of Divine transference of Moses' spirit to them.

What did this transference of spirit mean? It meant that the seventy elders did not and could not act on their own. Indeed, the meaning is that the seventy elders could not execute the assigned ministry except in the spirit of their leader, the one divinely placed over them, and by the power of the same. Moreover, when the seventy elders executed their ministry, when they prophesied without ceasing, they were doing so as representatives of their leader, Moses, and in the power of his spirit. Without Moses' spirit, the seventy elders could do nothing.

It is the contention here that the two passages cited above, viz., Exodus 18:13-33 and Numbers 11:16-17, 24-25, are indispensable in understanding Acts 6:1-7. Thus, we proceed in probing into what we believe to be the meaning of Acts 6:1-7 for the Black church.

THE MEANING OF ACTS 6:1-7 FOR A CHURCH OF POWER

As has been said earlier, the Early Church of the Acts of the Apostles was confronted with a crisis. That crisis was a growing conflict between Hebrew widows and Hellenist widows. The Hellenist widows felt they were neglected in the daily distribution of food and assistance while the Hebrew widows found favor.

Like Moses of Exodus and Numbers, the Twelve saw the need for assistance: "It is not reason that we should leave the word of God, and serve tables" (Acts 6:2b). The Black church is rife with conflict; always has been, and possibly always will be. Existence in a White racist society has made this so. There is no reason to think things will change dramatically for the better. Hence, there is a desperate need for pastoral assistance from the lay community in the church.

If there is any time in the history of the Black church when the Black preacher needs to give himself to prayer and the ministry of the Word of God, it is now. In the Black community of every city and community, there is a war in progress. That war is not in the streets or on a physical battlefield. The war is one of the mind and spirit of the people of the community. It is one to save and preserve them from demonic possession, social and spiritual contamination, and the utter effects of an historic slavery and endemic racism. There is the need for enlightened and Bible-oriented pastors to deal with this war and interpret for the people what "thus saith the Lord."

The situation is critical because there are only about three thousand Black preachers, pastors, theologians, and Christian educators of all denominations enrolled in Bible colleges, schools of theology, and divinity schools. There needs to be many, many more to give impetus to the intellectual warfare that is aloft in the Black church and surrounding community. Therefore, these who give themselves to prayer and the ministry of God's Word need to help in the execution of pastoral duties in the local church. However, the help need not come at the expense or compromise of pastoral authority in the local church and dilution of its spiritual power in the world.

This is where Acts 6:1-7 gives the Black church inestimable assistance and a boast to power. In Acts 6:3, the apostles direct the church to select seven men who bear the qualities of being full of the Holy Ghost, having wisdom, and a good report. Here, we have echoes of Exodus 18:21 when Moses' father-in-law, Jethro, gives the directive to his son-in-law to choose men to assist him who are 1) able, 2) God-fearing, 3) men of truth, and 4) men who hate covetousness.

In the Black church, those who assist the pastor need to be selected by the pastor. They need to possess the pastor's spirit and reflect his interests, concerns, and approach to the tasks of the church. If they do not conform to these characteristics, they should not be chosen. If it is not possible or practical for the pastor to choose deacons, those responsible for this extremely important action must do so by using guidelines provided and approved by the pastor. In the Old Testament passages cited above, Jethro, the priest, the preacher, gives to Moses the guidelines by which the men were to be chosen to assist in the ministry to the people (cf., Ex. 18:13-23). In Numbers 11:16-17, 24-25, it is God who gives directives to Moses as to how to choose the men upon whom God Himself will place Moses' spirit to assist in the ministry to the people. In Acts 6, the apostles give the directives as to the choice of the seven who are to help.

In Act 6, those who are chosen to be a part of the seven

are to be appointed over the business of the church by the apostles. Hence, in the Black church, when the pastor selects church members to assist him, he does not do so at the expense of his own authority or to dilute the power of the church.

Dr. Jacob Tileston Brown, erstwhile Director of Publications for the Sunday School Publishing Board, adamantly disagrees with the notion of a "deacon board" and a "chairman of deacons." Apparently, in the earlier part of this century, the R. B. C. Howell-born concept of a deacon board headed by a chairman (and that board being constituted of businessmen who were in charge of the business of the church) was wreaking havoc in the Black Baptist church. Dr. Brown sought to respond to the threat to National Baptist churches and put the controversy to rest in a book he called, *The Deacon Problem Solved*. His dedicatory statement in the front matter of the book reflects the serious nature of the damage this controversy was causing the Black Baptist church:

> To. . .the faithful pastors and their wives in general, throughout the Baptist denomination, who have experienced the ill effects, and who have suffered from this vital weakness in our polity. . . .[31]

From whom had we inherited this ecclesiastical malaise which wielded such "ill effects" and imposed on National Baptist churches a "vital weakness in our polity"? It is no question that such was inherited from the Howellian-born concept of deacons as constituting an official board with a chairman. These, according to R.B.C. Howell, were to be businessmen and were to be in charge of and responsible for all the business of the church. Under this arrangement, deacon boards and their chairmen

---

[31] Jacob Tileston Brown, *The Deacon Problem Solved*, (Nashville, Tennessee: Sunday School Publishing Board, 1928).

have come to have powerful political clout in the church. In fact, in many cases they have come to determine almost everything that goes on in the church. However, in the publication alluded to above, Dr. Brown understood Acts 6:1-7 to mean that deacons were needed because there was a job which needed to be done. Aside from that, they had no raison d'etre. Dr. Brown believed that through divine guidance, the seven deacons were set apart by the church with the sanction of the twelve apostles. He correctly pointed out in his book that once the crisis had passed and the needs of both the Hebrews and Hellenist widows met and the murmuring subsided, nothing more is heard of the deacons, only that they went off preaching themselves, e.g., Stephen and Philip. Dr. J. T. Brown wisely concluded that when a deacon successfully completed an assignment given by the pastor, he was no longer needed until the pastor gave another assignment.

Dr. Jacob Tileston Brown represents a serious pastoral mind-set of the early part of the century among National Baptists, as it relates to deacons and the full scope of pastoral duties. This mind-set was diametrically opposite from the church of the larger culture. For example, the late Dr. W. T. Crutcher, pastor of the Mt. Olive Baptist Church of Knoxville, Tennessee for fifty-four years never had a deacon board or an "ordained" deacon. With Acts 6:1-7 as his base of operation, his theory was that whenever he needed a task done by a deacon, he would appoint a man of the congregation to perform that task. He did not ordain him as such in order to sit on a board. For him, there was no need for a deacon board or a chairman. He needed deacons to help him, the pastor, do a job. Furthermore, once the man had completed the task, he no longer functioned in the capacity of deacon. Many National Baptist pastors from the "old school" held this pastoral philosophy and made it a functional component of church life.

CONCLUSION

From our brief study of Acts 6:1-7, we have discerned that there is no scriptural basis for an "official board of deacons." Neither is there Biblical justification for a "chairman of deacons." Such has come from the mind of man, not the mind of God. Further, we conclude from our inquiry that deacons have one job, and that is, as Dr. C.A.W. Clark of the Good Street Baptist Church, Dallas, Texas once mused, ". . .to help the pastor," and to do so in and with the spirit of the pastor upon them.

In one of our large metropolitan cities is a very successful congregation. This large assembly of Christians who worship as National Baptists have a wide assortment of effective programs and ministries. One of the deacons was asked what was the secret of their success and effectiveness. His response was that "If pastor . . . says to do it, you can consider it done; and, if he says not to do it, it is not going to be done." The inquirer said to the deacon, "Then there is no question about where authority lies in your church." The deacon rejoined, "That's right!" Thus, with no confusion of where authority lies in this church, that congregation is known for its powerful programs and ministries of uplift and help—activities which give hope to the people.

Another National Baptist congregation of a large midwest city enjoys a similar kind of honor and favor from God because the pastor gives courageous, imaginative, and unquestioned leadership, according to Acts 6:1-7. This congregation of Negro National Baptists operates a successful and effective school which religiously educates preschoolers and children up to the eighth grade. The school is so effective in its ministry of educating young children that there is a waiting list of more than thirteen hundred students.

It is exciting to see all the activity that goes on at that location. There are faculty members all about, church administrators working diligently, and children gleefully going about their business of learning in the security of the church building. Unavoidably, one discerns that the pastor is in full control. The men who surround him in the great work understand themselves, not as those who tell the pastor what to do or who run the church; but rather, they know their role as that of the pastor's helpers.

It is interesting to note that in the Acts account of the development of the Early Church, subsequent to Acts 6:1-7, there is not another similar kind of unrest within the congregation. In point of fact, the record states that after the seven were prayed over and had the hands of the apostles laid upon them, the church grew in power to the glory of God:

> And the word of God increased; and the number of disciples multiplied in Jerusalem greatly; and a great company of the priests were obedient to the faith. (Acts 6:7)

The Black church is too often hamstrung by leadership fights between the pastor and deacons. These exercises in ecclesiastical fisticuffs result in a church which is rendered pitifully impotent, ridiculously wretched, and hopelessly helpless when facing a restless sea of groping souls who are clutching and clawing for something onto which to hold in the quicksand of a very uncertain world. A rereading of Acts 6:1-7 helps us to know how to arrange our administrative apparatus and recognize the true relationship between pastor and deacons so we can once again become a church of power.

Chapter VI

POWER FOR THE CHURCH THROUGH COMMON SHARING ACCORDING TO ACTS 4:32

INTRODUCTION

Revolution most often takes place amid violence and hostility, bomb bursts, battalions, and batteries of artillery and ammunition. The Early Church effected a revolution, however, which was unequalled either then or now without any of these. A ripple hardly appeared on the proverbial bosom of the waters. Great power was wielded by the church by the sharing of resources by her members. The Early Church developed corporate power through the means of community sharing. In the Acts of the Apostles, we are introduced to the idea of members coexisting in the church. However, in chapter four of The Acts, we get a significant development regarding community sharing within the Early Church. In Acts 4:32, it is said that the membership of the church was of "one heart and one soul" ($\mathring{\eta}\nu\ \kappa\alpha\rho\delta\iota\alpha\ \kappa\alpha\iota\ \psi\upsilon\chi\mathring{\eta}\ \mu\iota\alpha$ = *ain kardia kai psuxai mia*), and none claimed any material thing as his/her own because they all had "everything in common" ($\pi\acute{\alpha}\nu\tau\alpha\ \kappa\omicron\iota\nu\acute{\alpha}$ = *panta koina*).

The result of having "everything in common" was not without great significance. Initially, great power was demonstrated among the people. Verse three of chapter four in The Acts states astoundingly that the Early Church gave their testimony of the resurrection of the Lord Jesus "with great power." The word used to describe the power that was demonstrated is *dunamei*, the same word which today is known for "dynamite." With dynamic, dynamite-like power, the early apostles testified of the resurrection of Jesus Christ. This came, however, only after they determined that they had everything in common.

Power to witness, which emerged out of oneness of mind and heart, evolved into the inevitable, willingness to share one's possessions with all other members of the church. Thus, verses 34ff., in chapter four in The Acts detail the results of this dynamic behavior which evolved out of oneness of mind and heart.

> There was not a needy person among them, for as many as were possessors of lands or houses sold them, and brought the proceeds of what was sold and laid it at the apostles' feet; and distribution was made to each as any had need. (Acts 4:34-35)

In the Early Church, everyone was cared for according to their need. There was no subsistence program provided by the government of the Roman Empire. That would have been nonsense, ipso facto, completely out of the question. There were many reasons for this. The first would probably be religion. The Roman Empire functioned on a religious premise. Like the Greek religious pantheon, the Roman religious pantheon was that of many gods. Most importantly, however, was what was known as the "Kaiser Kultus," i.e., worship of the Roman Caesar. To participate in any Roman government activity, including accepting government assistance, would mean engaging in the religious rites of the government. (An example would be the implicit challenge which Jesus put to the Pharisees and Herodians when He said, "Render to Caesar the things that are Caesar's and to God the things that are God's" Mark 12:17 RSV.)

Throughout the Acts of the Apostles, there is a definite emphasis on the Early Church's refusal to worship her human leaders. A good example of this is found in Acts 10:25f., when the Roman centurion Cornelius, fell at Peter's feet to worship him.

> When Peter entered, Cornelius met him and fell down at his feet and worshiped him. But Peter lifted him up, saying, "Stand up; I too am a man." (Acts 10:25, 26 RSV)

Peter's refusal to allow Cornelius to bow before him is indicative of the Early Church's denial of such idolatry as part of its spiritual posture (also, see Revelation 19:10). If the Early Church had accepted assistance from Roman government officials, in effect, they would be part and parcel participants in idolatrous worship inasmuch as it was obligatory to do obeisance before Roman officials, especially the Emperor, even the statues representing them, as an expression of allegiance and worship as divine.

Another more obvious reason the Early Church would refuse to accept assistance from the Roman government is that to do so rendered them subject to Roman authority. This is another way of saying if you dance to the music, you have to pay the piper.

Today's church faces similar challenges in her relations with the federal government. Like the Roman government, there is a religious aura about the United States of America. H. Richard Niebuhr calls it the nation with the soul of a church. Martin Marty referred to it as "the righteous empire." Our beloved country is the eager recipient of the politico-religious institutions of the Greco/Roman/British Empires. The sacred nature of the flag is a good example. In the Roman Empire, to pass a flag or bust of a Roman Emperor without bowing or saluting was sacrilegious and punishable by imprisonment, beating, or death. The entire court system of America is built on the religious principles of the Greco/Roman/British legal systems. In those ancient legal court systems, especially the Roman system, the Emperor served as the Pontifex Maximus and Chief Magistrate. He served as the highest representative of the gods; he was, ipso facto, a god himself. Thus, when the judge entered the courtroom, those in the room are told "All rise!" because "His Honor" the judge is entering. Not to do so could result in being charged with contempt of court. Similarly, when lawyers approached the bench, they addressed the judge by saying, "I pray, thee, Sir!" The assumption was that, the Emperor being god, appeal had to be made to him that he might execute his spiritual authority in the petitioner's favor. The contemporary church and her members must realize that this is what transpires when appearance is made before a court in America.

Restrictions and limitations are not so evident today in terms of Christians observing their Faith. Persecutions and death are not imposed upon devotees of the Christian Faith as was the case in the Roman Empire. However, there are implicit as well as explicit problems with the church's relation to the federal government. One of the problems is that of the government's ever-increasing authority over the church. This is especially true when the government makes available sums of money to the church or joins it in some dual venture. This kind of relationship opens the door for government inquiry into the financial and personal affairs of the church. If grants are made for employment programs, housing developments, food distribution and feeding programs, the government automatically gains entrée into the affairs of the church, breaching the privacy and autonomy of the church. Any time a joint venture is entered with the government, the church must be aware of this great risk. Surely the church has nothing to hide from anyone, including the federal government; however, there is still the fundamental principle of separation of church and state, a foundation stone of our nation, with which we must honestly deal.

The Early Church rejected the Roman Empire's religious aura and influence over it and cut off that legal authority by rejecting its amenities and courtesies (if indeed there were any). The Early Church was the epitome of separation of church and state. It really stretches the imagination to think that financial assistance might have been available from the Roman Empire. As has been stated elsewhere in this writing, hardly any overtures would have been made by the Roman government toward the church, because the Christian church was an illegal entity in the land. The existence of the Early Church was indeed an act of rebellion against the Roman Empire. To be a part of a group which preached about a "Kingdom of God" was to be a part of a treasonous crowd. But by sharing financial resources and substance from field to food with each other and resisting the Roman government, the Early Church built for herself a base of power.

TOGETHERNESS AS A PREREQUISITE FOR A SHARING CHURCH

There is much evidence in the New Testament which sustains the importance of prayer in the life of the Early Church. Such activity, it is revealed, wrought great effects, especially in terms of togetherness and power.

Let us begin with the first chapter of The Acts. In verse six, when the disciples asked Jesus, ". . .will you at this time restore the kingdom to Israel?" it is said that "they had come together" ($\sigma \upsilon \nu \epsilon \lambda \theta \acute{o} \nu \tau \epsilon \varsigma$ = *sunelthontes*). The disciples did not come to Jesus one at a time, dragging in as a ragtag gang; they came together. Returning from the Mount of Olives and going to the Upper Room in Jerusalem, the disciples of Jesus assembled. Once again, Luke places emphasis on "togetherness." "All these with one accord devoted themselves to prayer *together* [ὁμοθυμαδὸν = *homothumadon*] with the women and Mary the mother of Jesus, and with his brothers" (cf., Acts 1:14 RSV, emphasis mine). This togetherness marked the orderliness of the replacement of Judas within the circle of disciples (cf., Acts 1:15ff).

When the Day of Pentecost came, Luke reports that "...they were all together [ὁμοῦ = *homou*] in one place" when the Holy Spirit came upon the assembly like the blast of a mighty wind (cf., Acts 2:2). Although the Lukan expression of *homothumadon* is not used in Acts 3:1ff., it is clear that Peter and John went up together (Πέτρος δὲ καὶ Ἰωάννης ἀνέβαινον = *Petros de kai Ioannes anebainon*) at the hour of prayer. The result of their togetherness was the healing of a man who had laid daily at the temple gate called Beautiful.

Luke's emphasis on prayer and togetherness sets the stage for a church membership which unhesitatingly and unilaterally shares all their resources with one another—a most radical proposition for the contemporary church. A look at Acts 2:43ff., will demonstrate how intensely faithful the Early Church was to the ideology and theology of complete sharing.

THE PLACE OF FEAR IN THE SHARING CHURCH

In verse forty-three of chapter two in The Acts, Luke begins with the expression that "...fear came upon every soul." When you study Luke's theology, you will discover a definite place for fear in his theological scheme.

In all of his disclosure of God's dramatic intervention into the affairs of men, "fear" plays a very important part. Upon God's revelation of the birth of John the Baptist to his father Zechariah, Luke reports that "fear" fell upon him at the time of the visit of the angel of the Lord (cf., Luke 1:12). Similarly, at the annunciation of the birth of Jesus (Lk. 1:29ff), Mary is said to be "greatly troubled" at the saying of the angel Gabriel. Gabriel rejoined that Mary should "...not be afraid" (Lk. 1:30 RSV).

The shepherds of chapter two are another example of Luke's employment of fear as a response to God's divine activity, an act which elicits a positive reaction. The incident was the angel's announcement of the birth of Jesus.

> And in that region there were shepherds out in the field, keeping watch over their flock by night. And an angel of the Lord appeared to them, and the glory of the Lord shone around them, and they were filled with fear. (Luke 2:8f RSV)

Fear, the kind which is elicited when God intervenes in history in what Paul Tillich calls a "kairotic moment" is one of the ingredients which cultivated an attitude of common sharing within the κοινωνία = *koinonia*, the fellowship of the Early Church.

> And fear came upon every soul; and many wonders and signs were done through the apostles. And all who believed were together and had all things in common; and they sold their possessions and goods and distributed them to all, as any had need. (Acts 2:43ff RSV)

The dimension of fear is one to be seriously considered if the contemporary church is to resume its posture of power as was the case with her predecessor in the Biblical era. Acknowledgement of dramatic acts of God in the midst of men and a fearful response to the same could mean the emergence of a church given to sharing resources among her members. Failure to do so, i.e., to fearfully acknowledge God's acts in history, could mean in all likelihood, a church given to selfishness, greed, and self-aggrandizement.

There is no question about the dynamic movement of God in the world. In recent years, God thumped the earth in the nation of Armenia so much so that an entire city was leveled and hundreds of thousands of human beings were killed amid crumbling buildings and yawning chasms in the ground swallowing up helpless victims. In one year, 1989, on the east coast of the United States, Hurricane Hugo crashed into the city of Charleston, South Carolina, crippling it in ways unknown in years before. On the west coast of the nation, a severe earthquake shook the San Francisco/Oakland, California Bay Area and wrought devastation which only could be the result of the divine hand of God. But such divine intervention has failed to elicit the kind of fear which characterized the Early Church. Life goes on as usual. Only for a moment, when the Persian Gulf War erupted and Saddam Hussein momentarily threatened the world with Armageddon, was there some evidence of fear among the faithful. However, swift victory by America and a coalition of military forces from around the world brought that momentary fear to euphoria and glee over the military power of America.

Fear of God! It must become anew a characteristic of the contemporary Black church. It must be as Herman Melville's character Starbuck in *Moby Dick*, when he says that he will have no sailor on his ship who does not fear the great fish, the whale. God is greater than any big fish. God must be feared! The Scripture avers that "Behold, the fear of the Lord, that is wisdom" (Job 28:28). Fear of the divine God of the universe is prerequisite for the people of God who willingly share their possessions with fellow believers.

THE POWER OF PRAYER IN SHARING

Prayer is another inextricably important component if the Black church is to become a power as the result of being a sharing membership. Prayer is prominent in the theology of the Acts of the Apostles. Wherever there are demonstrations of power in the Acts, the church has been engaged in prayer. When they chose the replacement of Judas, the church prayed (cf., Acts 1:24). In Acts 2:42ff., the church experienced great wonders and signs at the hands of the apostles, the membership was *together*, and God added to the church daily ". . .such as should be saved" because the membership ". . .continued stedfastly in the apostles' doctrine and fellowship, and in breaking of bread, and *the prayers*" (emphasis mine). Peter and John healed a lame man laying at the Beautiful Gate as they were going up to the temple ". . .at the hour of *prayer*" (emphasis mine). There is no greater demonstration of the power of prayer than in Acts 16 when Paul and Silas burst forth from jail by no force other than that of communication with God in prayer. Paul and Silas were unjustly charged with teaching customs unlawful to Roman law. The truth was that they had cast out from a young woman a spirit of divination to the displeasure of her owners whose gain from her services had been jeopardized. The Scripture says that while in jail, Paul and Silas prayed at midnight. Their prayers evoked the power of God to quake the earth until the foundations of the prison shook and the doors flew open, and the captives were set free.

In the Acts of the Apostles, the case is powerfully made that there is power in prayer. Prayer is indeed one of the indispensable components of a congregation's life if her members effectively share of their resources with one another. Hence, prayer, togetherness, and fear of God were all functional in the life of the Early Church in effecting a posture of sharing resources one member with another.

Breach of any of these components signaled certain death to any member of the church guilty of the infraction. In the fifth chapter of the Acts of the Apostles, the story is told of Ananias and his wife Sapphira. Their failure to honor the above led them to dishonesty. They sold a piece of their property and only reported to the church a portion of the revenue received (cf., Acts 5:1ff). Both Ananias and wife Sapphira died and were buried in shame for refusing to share with the church all the proceeds from the sale of their land.

It is clear that in the Acts of the Apostles that individualism and self-aggrandizement were not consonant with a church of power. Contradistinctively, such was reason for eminent death wrought by the Holy Spirit. On the contrary, the church of the Acts of the Apostles grew in economic strength and subsequently political strength because it was financially independent and strong, ipso facto, a church of power. That independence was due to the fact that every member shared equally of his possessions.

The passage in the Acts which profoundly expresses this is found in Acts 4:31ff. All of the components, viz., prayer, togetherness, and fear of God are present here. The result is that there was great alacrity among the membership to share their possessions with one another. The passage reads:

> And when they had prayed, the place in which they were gathered together was shaken; and they were all filled with the Holy Spirit and spoke the word of God

with boldness. Now the company of those who believed were of one heart and soul, and no one said that any of the things which he possessed was his own, but they had everything in common. And with great power the apostles gave their testimony to the resurrection of the Lord Jesus, and great grace was upon them all. There was not a needy person among them, for as many as were possessors of lands or houses sold them, and brought the proceeds of what was sold and laid it at the apostles' feet; and distribution was made to each as any had need. (Acts 4:31-35 RSV)

CONTEMPORARY APPLICATION

At the inception of this discussion, we posited the notion that it was unthinkable that the Early Church of the Acts of the Apostles would have accepted financial assistance from the Roman government. Certainly, there would not have been applications made for the same by the church. The fact that the Early Church was an illegal entity in the Roman society and each member subject to imprisonment, persecution, and death as a result of their membership in the church, made it illogical, impractical, unwise, and unsafe to do any of the above. For the most domesticated church, government assistance would have robbed it of its independence, freedom, and consonant power. The Early Church of the New Testament simply would not have been a church of power, surely as we read of it therein, had the Roman government some hand in its financial support. It was difficult enough after the church overwhelmed the Roman Empire in the fourth century (ca., A.D. 325) when Emperor Constantine domesticated Christianity and adopted her religion, holy days, and all that went with Christianity. The church of that era did all it could to prevent the Roman Empire from dominating it to the point of fuzzying its distinctives and graying its characteristics and rendering it impotent to fight against evil.

The same care must be taken today as it relates to government assistance and private funding sources to benefit the church. For the contemporary church to be the CHURCH OF POWER as was its predecessor in the Acts of the Apostles, her membership must resume the practice of sharing resources with one another and giving what is due to God.

As Scripture, the Acts of the Apostles gives us a fresh script, a clear road map, an accurate blueprint for restructuring a contemporary church which demonstrates power through sharing among her members. Inquiry into the text herein discloses the kinds of inventory items which are musts for this kind of church of power. The inventory items needed are: 1) the church must be given to prayer, 2) the membership must be together, 3) the membership must stand in fear of the presence of the Holy Spirit and His dynamic effect upon them, 4) the soul and heart of the membership must be in union (cf., Acts 4:31f). If the contemporary Black church were to check its inventory and assure the placement of these characteristics, surely the resulting benefits as seen in the life of the Early Church would emerge.

One of the major benefits demonstrated in the Early Church of the Acts of the Apostles was that of a powerful witness regarding the resurrection of the Lord Jesus. The power and authenticity of the church is greatly dependent upon the congregation's stewardship of their possessions. There is something extremely hollow in the hallowed worship of a people, their animated movements while ostensibly under the power of the "Holy Ghost," their shouts, their holy dances, speaking in tongues, and the like, when there is no complimenting demonstration of stewardship of money, talent, and time. There is something greatly wrong when a congregation comes together to "have church," to "praise the Lord," to "let the Holy Spirit have His way," and the worship place is battered and broken and in need of desperate repair. Something is amiss when a church's records fail to disclose missionary concern for the poor and destitute in every place. A congregation cannot claim power and efficacy if its fiscal resources are not inclusive of monies set aside for scholarships for the education of the youth in her midst and leadership training for church leaders. If a congregation is not engaged in amassing fiscal resources to provide its needy members shelter, food, raiment, employment, etc., there is little about which the people can rejoice.

Moreover, if the only reason a congregation comes together is "to have a good time in the Lord," already that group of people has abdicated their raison d'etre, their reason for being. And surely, their testimony of the resurrection of the Lord Jesus, if indeed this is even on their lips, has a hollow ring and empty feeling. The Early Church, because of her courage to be and to demonstrate that being by way of sharing resources one member with another, wielded great power in their witness of the resurrection of Jesus Christ.

The contemporary Black church can hardly continue in its state of being smitten by a terrible malaise of weakness. The plight of the people begs for a Black church which will be honest and responsible with her fiscal resources. What we hazard is a curse upon our people because we have not given what is due to God and equitably shared our financial resources for the uplift of our people. The frightening reality of what happens when a people believe not God and respond in kind with repentance and obedience is seen in the history of the cities of Chorazin,

Bethsaida, and Capernaum in Galilee of Israel. These three cities were the places where, according to the Gospel of Matthew, "...most of [Jesus'] mighty works were done," but "...they repented not" (Mt. 11:20). A full casting of the text would best do justice to the woes which Jesus pronounced against these cities because of their unbelief.

> Woe unto thee, Chorazin! woe unto thee, Bethsaida! for if the mighty works, which were done in you, had been done in Tyre and Sidon, they would have repented long ago in sackcloth and ashes. But I say unto you, It shall be more tolerable for Tyre and Sidon at the day of judgment, than for you. And thou, Capernaum, which art exalted unto heaven, shalt be brought down to hell: for if the mighty works, which have been done in thee, had been done in Sodom, it would have remained until this day. But I say unto you, That it shall be more tolerable for the land of Sodom in the day of judgment, than for thee. (Mt. 11:21-24)

These three cities were thriving centers in the vicinity of the Sea of Galilee. In the time of Jesus, Capernaum, for instance, was a bustling village of fishermen, with a population of about 10,000 to 15,000. Simon Peter and his family lived there. It is there that Jesus began his Galilean Ministry, casting out a demon-possessed man from the synagogue and healing Simon's mother-in-law of a fever. But in all Jesus did in those cities, they believed not and refused to repent of their sins. If one were to visit those cities today, they would not be found. Only the rubble of their previous existence remains. In an earthquake of A.D. 749 which struck in the African-Syrian Rift in Israel, all three of these cities were leveled to the ground. To this day, neither of them has been rebuilt. This fulfills the prophecy of Jesus and the result of his woes.

It is unquestionable that Black people in America have had some of the most dramatic things to happen which only could be attributed to acts of God. From the time of the enslavement of Black people in America until now, there are incidents in our history which only can be attributed to acts of God. Thus, there should be an outpouring of gratitude to God and commitment to His cause on the part of Black people. Moreover, there should be tangible demonstrations of this gratitude which manifest themselves in the abundant sharing of fiscal resources with one another in the church. Not to do so invites the curse of God. Malachi 3:9 hovers over the head of the Black church with the threat of woe and conviction. God says,

> You are cursed with a curse, for you have robbed me, even this whole nation. (NKJV)

In Malachi 3:9, the curse is upon the people for, as God says in the text, "Ye have robbed me. . . . In tithes and offerings" (Mal. 3:8).

Because of the merciful nature of God, however, there needs to be no curse upon Black people and the Black church today. This is true because the curse is lifted when God's people recommit themselves to honesty before Him and give what is due Him, the tithe and offering. The benefits are remarkable:

1) Blessings from the windows of heaven, the volume of which the recipient is unable to handle (*see*, Mal. 3:9)
2) The devil, the devourer, will be rebuked
3) The fruit of one's ground will not be destroyed
4) One's fruit will not be cast in the field before time
5) The people shall be called blessed of all nations
6) The people shall be a delightsome land.

Aside from what is cited here, the Biblical mandate of tithing carries with it some wonderful benefits as far as monetary capability of the church to meet human needs is concerned. Let us take, for example, a Baptist association with a membership of thirty churches. If each church had a membership on the average of 250 members and each member of the church tithed at least $25, assuming each member had an average income of about $250 per week, the gross tithes received for the week would be $6,250. If each of the thirty churches tithed to the association, the total tithes received for that Sunday alone would be $18,750. If this were done each of the fifty-two Sundays in the year, the total amount of tithes received from all churches in the association would be $975,000. The figures would look like this:

	250	No. of mbrs. in ea. church
$	x 25.00	Amt. of tithe per member
$	6,250.00	Total tithes rec'd per church ea. week
$	625.00	Total tithe rec'd in Assoc. per church
	x30	No. of churches in the Assoc.
$	18,750.00	Total rec'd in Assoc. for one Sunday
$	18,750.00	Total rec'd in Assoc. for one Sunday
	x52	
$975,000.00		Total tithes rec'd by Assoc. from churches for one year.

If these association churches were to give a tenth of the tithe to missions, education, and employment of persons needing jobs, there would be $975,000 available to do the work. This is, it should be kept in mind, only for one Black Baptist association. If we were to utilize this formula on a national level, e.g., for the National Baptist Convention, USA, Inc., the numbers would be staggering. If, for example, we took an average National Baptist Convention, USA, Inc., congregation made up of an average of 250 members with a total tithe offering each Sunday of $6,250, and multiplied it by the number of churches in the convention, the figures would look like this for an average weekly generation of revenue.

$$\begin{array}{r} \$6{,}250.00 \\ \times\ 35000 \\ \hline \$218{,}750{,}000.00 \end{array}$$

If this $218,750,000 were computed over a year's time, the National Baptist Convention, USA, Inc., would generate and place in banks annually, the sum of $11,375,000,000.

$$\begin{array}{r} \$218{,}750{,}000.00 \text{ amt gen'd by NBC churches} \\ \underline{52} \text{ wks. in the year} \end{array}$$

Total $11,375,000,000.00 potential intake of NBC chs.

A tithe of this amount would be over $1.1 billion.

If this formula from the Old Testament were to be utilized, the plight of Black people in general and Black Baptists in particular would be far different—in a positive sense. Our children could be educated through our own resources; our elderly persons could be cared for out of our own substance; employment could be provided for our own people, young and older; the needy could be cared for with dignity; and healthcare could be provided for all. This is the plan given from the Old Testament, one which worked for the people of the Old Testament for centuries and could work for us now.

So many members of the contemporary Black church, however, have serious problems with the Old Testament mandate to tithe. The reasons are myriad. They all seem to emerge out of some conclusion that such requirement is a burden. Strangely enough, many Black Baptists tacitly oppose tithing because of what they think is the Old Testament's teaching about it, viz., that a portion of it is given to the priest or, for us, the preacher, the pastor. What indeed the Old Testament book of Leviticus teaches is that the priest and his family, sons, were to eat the tithe offering, e.g., the cereal offering and sin offering (*see,* Lev. 6:14, 24; *et passim*). Hence, this mindset is based purely on error, eisegetical proclivity, and prejudice. The effect of this failure to "do it God's way," is that the Black Baptist church continues in a less than powerful posture.

As we look at the church of power in the Acts of the Apostles, we can clearly see a Christian fellowship which demanded far more of its members than at any time in the Old Testament Era. As has been cited above, not a member of the nascent Early Church fellowship counted any of their possessions as their own (cf., Acts 4:32). Each sold all they had and gave to a common fund for distribution throughout the membership (cf., Acts 2:44f). Fear of divine judgment kept any from violating this obligation. The result of such practice was phenomenal as it pertained to the overall membership—none had need! (cf., Acts 4:34f).

The contemporary Black Baptist church must move to empower herself through the adoption of Biblical models of economic development. Like the Early Church of the Acts of the Apostles, the end result will be a church which will be both financially independent as well as politically and socially powerful. There will be no need to subscribe to grants and financial assistance from the federal government, thus suffering the strains and restraints, embarrassment and spiritual impotence which accompany such union. In a very real sense, we will become the church of power.

BIBLIOGRAPHY

Barrett, C. K. *Luke the Historian in Recent Study*. Facets Books. Biblical Series No. 24. Philadelphia: Fortress Press, 1970.

Beare, Frank W. "Greek Religion". In *The Interpreter's Dictionary of the Bible*. Vol. 3. George A. Buttrick, ed. Nashville: Abingdon Press, 1962.

Black, Matthew. "Pharisees". In *The Interpreter's Dictionary of the Bible*. George A. Buttrick, ed. Vol. 3. Nashville: Abingdon Press, 1962.

Blaiklock, E. M. *The Acts of the Apostles*. Vol. 5 of *Tyndale New Testament Commentaries*. Grand Rapids, Michigan: Wm. B. Eerdmans Publishing Company, 1959.

Bruce, F. F. *The Acts of the Apostles*. Grand Rapids, Michigan: Eerdmans Publishing Company, 1951.

———. "Acts of the Apostles." In *The International Standard Bible Encyclopedia*. Geoffrey W. Bromiley, ed. Vol. 1. Grand Rapids, Michigan: William B. Eerdmans Publishing Company, 1979.

Cadbury, Henry J. "Acts of the Apostles." In *The Interpreter's Dictionary of the Bible*. George Arthur Buttrick, ed. Vol. 1. Nashville: Abingdon Press, 1962.

Cassidy, Richard J. *Society and Politics in the Acts of the Apostles*. Orbis Books: Maryknoll, New York, 1987.

Clark, A. C. *The Acts of the Apostles*. Oxford: Clarendon Press, 1933.

Conzelman, Hans. *Theology of St. Luke*. Trans. by Geoffrey Buswell. Philadelphia: Fortress Press, 1961.

Dibelius, Martin. *Studies in the Acts of the Apostles*. Trans. by Mary Ling. New York: Scribner's Sons, 1956.

Eusebius Pamphilus. *The Ecclesiastical History*. Trans. by Christian Frederick Cruse. Grand Rapids, Michigan: Baker Book House, 1955.

Fitzmyer, Joseph. *The Gospel According To Luke I-IX*. In *The Anchor Bible*. William Foxwell Albright and David Noel Freedman, ed. Garden City, New York: Doubleday & Company, Inc., 1981.

Fuller, Reginald H. *A Critical Introduction to the New Testament*. Studies in Theology. Letchworth, Hertfordshire: The Garde City Press Limited, 1966.

Grant, Michael. *The World of Rome*. A Mentor Book. New York: New American Library, 1960.

Grant, Robert M. *A Historical Introduction to the New Testament*. A Touchstone Book. New York: Simon and Schuster, 1972.

Haenchen, Ernst. *The Acts of the Apostles*. Trans. by Bernard Noble and Gerald Shinn. Philadelphia: The Westminster Press, 1971.

Harnack, Adolf von. *The Acts of the Apostles*. Trans. by J. R. Wilkinson. London: Williams & Norgate, 1909.

———. *The Mission and Expansion of Christianity*. Trans. and Edit. by James Moffatt. Gloucester, Massachusetts: Peter Smith, 1972.

Jackson, F. J. Foakes and Lake, Kirsopp, eds. *The Acts of the Apostles in the Beginnings of Christianity*. 5 Volumes. Grand Rapids, Michigan: Baker Book House, 1979.

Keck, Leander E. and Martyn, J. Louis, eds. *Studies in Luke-Acts*. Nashville: Abingdon Press, 1966.

Kümmel, Werner Georg, ed. *Introduction to the New Testament*. Trans. by A. J. Mattill, Jr. Nashville: Abingdon Press, 1966.

Leaney, A. R. C. *The Gospel according to St. Luke*. Second Edition In Black's New Testament Commentaries. London: Adam & Charles Black, 1958.

Macgregor, G. H. C. *The Acts of the Apostles*. Vol 9 of *The Interpreter's Bible*. Edit. by George A. Buttrick. Nashville: Abingdon Press, 1954.

Marxsen, Willi. *Introduction to the New Testament*. Trans. by G. Buswell. Philadelphia: Fortress Press, 1970.

Munck, Johannes. *The Acts of the Apostles*. Vol 31 of *The Anchor Bible*. Revised by William F. Albright and C. S. Mann. Garden City, New York: Doubleday & Company, Inc., 1967.

Plummer, Alfred. *The Gospel according to St. Luke*. In *The International Critical Commentary*. Fifth Edition. Edinburgh: T. & T. Clark, 38 George Street, 1901.

Ramsay, William M. *St. Paul the Traveller and the Roman Citizen*. Grand Rapids, Michigan: Baker Book House, 1977.

Suetonius. *Lives of the Caesars*. Trans. by J. C. Rolfe. No. 38 of *Loeb Classical Library*. Cambridge, Massachusetts: Harvard University Press, 1970.

Tacitus. *Annals*. Trans. by J. Jackson. No. 322 of *Loeb Classical Library*. Cambridge, Massachusetts: Harvard University Press, 1969.

Torrey, C. C. *The Composition and Date of Acts*. Cambridge: Harvard University Press, 1916.

Wilson, S. G. *The Gentiles and the Gentile Mission In Luke-Acts*. No. 23 of *Society For New Testament Studies Monograph Series*. Cambridge: At The University Press, 1973.